Mark Gibbard SSJE

Why Pray?

SCM PRESS LTD

334 01791 2

First published 1970
by SCM Press Ltd
56 Bloomsbury Street London WC1

© *SCM Press Ltd 1970*

Printed in Great Britain by
Billing & Sons Limited
Guildford and London

scm centrebooks

Christianity at the Centre/John Hick
Who is God?/D. W. D. Shaw
What about the Old Testament?/John Bowden
What is the New Testament?/T. G. A. Baker
What is the Church?/Victor de Waal
What is Right?/Michael Keeling
The Last Things Now/David L. Edwards
Who is Jesus Christ?/A. O. Dyson
What about the Children?/John Gray
Who is a Christian?/John Bowden

Contents

Introduction

All kinds of people are now finding prayer a problem; out of conversations with them this short book has almost written itself. There are many people who now pray very much less than they used to do and pray with far less conviction; and some of them are men and women doing responsible work in the churches. They live with questions and doubts. 'Why should I bother to pray?' they say, 'for no obvious reason prayer has gone dead for me.' Then sometimes there is a sigh of relief, when I explain that they are not alone with this problem; it is not new, it has been with us for centuries. Yet this does not make it any less pressing, and it needs to be dealt with in the idiom of today.

I also meet people deeply involved in serving and helping others, and they ask in genuine concern, 'Would prayer really add anything effective to what we are already doing? And there is so much that must be done. Why waste valuable time on prayer?'

Behind this question there is often a lurking doubt, 'And can we in fact be sure of God?' This problem seems to crop up in two ways. On the one hand, for some people it is not primarily an intellectual matter. They almost inhale doubt with the atmosphere in which they have to live and earn their living. So much of their surroundings makes the suggestion, 'Is there God? Who can be sure? At any rate he does not seem to do anything for you. So live for the things that are real to you.' All this by-passes their reasoning, it seems to me, but it penetrates their lives, influences what they do, and makes prayer look foolish.

On the other hand, for some their doubts are much more

intellectual. The stark fact of evil and suffering makes it apparent to them that, even if there should be a God, he either cannot or will not intervene to help us. So prayer is futile. Then many people today are so overwhelmed by the immense size and age of the universe, disclosed by modern science, that they ask themselves, 'How can any creator-deity concern himself with the needs of millions of infinitesimal human beings on this tiny planet? So why bother to pray?'

There is the further problem raised by linguistic analysis, which examines precisely and critically the language we use and its reference to any supposed reality. This analysis has been prevalent now in many philosophical circles for a generation. It has sharply posed the issue of whether the word 'God' is in any sense a meaningful term; while at the same time the traditional reasons given for believing in God have come under much heavier fire. Although the apparent crudity of the first formulations of linguistic analysis has changed, the 'God-question' is still posed. Many believers in God feel acutely threatened by it, and consequently for them the reality has gone out of prayer.

For some years I had sensed that prayer was becoming a nagging problem for many people, but I did not realize how widespread this had become until I listened to a report about worship and prayer being passed by the Fourth Assembly of the World Council of Churches in July 1968, at the Swedish university city of Uppsala. Official representatives had come from over two hundred churches in eighty countries. Their report stated:

> We know how deeply the question of worship troubles many as a personal anxiety. Some Christians seek to maintain a rhythm of personal prayer, despite repeated lapses. Some are nostalgic for the reality of prayer, as the presence of God in prayer becomes less and less real to them. Most feel guilty about their lack of prayer. Some have almost given up the effort to pray.[1]

Yet in spite of all this bewilderment and doubt, I think I see some evidence on the other side. For example, I have been surprised in these last few months at how many people are considering prayer almost for the first time. These are not giving it up; they are trying to start. Some have been brought up with nothing but the vaguest ideas of religion; some have rebelled with some justification against the dreary drill of an 'establishment' religion; most of them are still very vague about God, yet they have a hunch that there may be something in prayer. They sense that praying might make them more sensitive to others and more resilient in their work and service. Many students, who are opposed to society and to religion as these are now, and who are often actively involved in political and social change, are hungry for some kind of spiritual experience. This has struck me forcibly. Sometimes they try to satisfy this hunger in what look to be strange ways. Some, for example, look towards eastern mysticism, because nearly always the church of the west seems to them spiritually bankrupt and dead.

> The signs of this quest are easy to see; courses on religion are most popular on a growing number of campuses; activist demonstrations and hippie be-ins have become for young people the contemporary equivalent of religious rites and celebrations. Students are, in short, less convinced that 'God is dead' than the radical theologians are.[2]

Although I have had for years the privilege of sharing in a community life with a regular rhythm of prayer, I now feel that I am hardly more than at the beginning of finding out what praying really is. I have many friends to thank, young and old, from many backgrounds, who have spoken with me of their difficulties and discoveries in prayer. I am particularly grateful to a group of friends in Oxford engaged in teaching and in work among students. For three years we have met, we have read papers, discussed and rewritten them. We began by thinking about how we could advise others, but very soon we found the problem was in ourselves. If there are any insights in this book relevant to the present day, I owe them largely to these friends. For the last few months I have also had the pleasure and stimulus of living among students in the United States and have seen new aspects of the problem of prayer. And what a time it has been!

As I write these lines, I look back over these experiences with gratitude and bewilderment. I recall conversations I have had, listening to people's difficulties in prayer. I have reflected on books I have read; some of them have put these difficulties even more sharply. I could not help sometimes feeling these problems on my own pulse. I have experienced the doubts I try to meet. What I now write is provisional. I am trying to explore what praying is.

Oxford 1970

NOTES

1. *Uppsala Report*, Geneva: WCC 1968, p. 78.
2. Myron B. Bloy, Jr (ed.), *Multi-Media Worship*, New York: Seabury 1969, p. 5.

1 Praying is Exploration

Can we even begin?

Seldom has there been such real concern for our fellow-men and women, not least among students. There are the protests against the horrors of war and against the uncalled-for intervention of the great powers whether of the left or of the right. There are the demands that the hunger, poverty and frustrations of the underprivileged should be swept away both in the 'third world' of Asia, Africa, and South America, and also in the ghettoes and pockets of poverty among the affluent countries of the west. There are struggles against unjust racial discrimination. There is the claim for educational reform, so that no one's abilities should remain undiscovered and undeveloped, and that new ways of education from kindergarten to university and beyond should be explored. Beneath all this action there is the fundamental demand that men and women should no longer be caught up into a ruthless competitive society, but rather that, across all our barriers, we should accept completely and equally all our fellow human beings as brothers and sisters (how we all experience this as a tough unceasing demand!), and so at last live together in true 'humanness'. The achievements of our technology are putting this within our grasp, though we do not close our eyes to the defects and dangers in our society.

Concern about man and unconcern about God. Demand for action and disregard of prayer. Yet at odd moments there is a strange groping towards some more-than-human experience and an enquiring into what that really might be.

There are plenty of enquirers about praying, though often rather tentative enquirers. Some feel like giving up prayer, yet they cannot bring themselves to stop praying altogether and they ask advice about it rather despairingly. Others ask about it because they are starting from practically zero or trying to give it another trial after years without prayer. Nearly all of them feel that, if they could pray with intellectual honesty, this might bring something into their own lives, it might somehow link them to others whom they admire and love, and it might help in their personal relationships. What often opens their eyes to such possibilities is meeting people whose attractiveness and authenticity they sense to be rooted in genuine prayer.

Sometimes it may be an individual. Teilhard de Chardin, the Jesuit scientist, had this kind of influence. A fellow-Jesuit, who shared his exacting life in China, said of Teilhard:

> The look in his eyes when they met your eyes revealed the man's soul; his reassuring sympathy restored your confidence in yourself. Just to speak to him made you feel better; you knew he was listening to you and he understood you. His own faith was in the invincible power of love.[1]

This gift was not merely his natural *bonhomie*, but sprang from his deep life of prayer, which you can feel pulsating in his letters and especially in his thought-provoking book on prayer, *Le Milieu Divin*.

On the other hand, sometimes it may be the shared life of a group of believers that starts others enquiring about prayer. Here is a personal experience. Some years ago I met a group of this kind living in a dilapidated house by an oil refinery near Marseilles. They were workers at the refinery, and at the same time they were members of one of the most pioneering religious orders, inspired by Charles de Foucauld, an army officer, turned Trappist, turned Sahara hermit.[2] You would never guess that they were members of a religious community. They were dressed like the other workers in the district. Their one downstairs room was always 'open house'. On the door was written, 'Come in without knocking'. All sorts of people used to turn up. You could hardly believe your eyes when you saw some of the men sitting round their table for their frugal, rather hilarious evening meal. They were not the kind of men who would go to any religious meeting. Upstairs there were only two rooms. One room had a couple of camp beds; the third brother had another camp bed under the stairs. Many people in the neighbourhood knew that the other tiny room upstairs was a chapel. There every morning they had a simple mass and every evening the brothers had an hour's silent prayer. Whenever I shared in this time of prayer, it was a strange experience. There was incessant noise outside, but oddly enough this seemed to drive you to prayer rather than distract you from prayer. Somehow you sensed that the steady rhythm of prayer in this setting was the secret of the brothers. It was this that helped to make them so open to this largely dechristianized world and so understanding of its deeper needs. My few days with them was one of the events of my life. I know that I am far from being the only one whose eyes were opened by that house to more of the reality of prayer.

Doubtless there are other influences as well which lead people to enquire about prayer, even while they are still very unsure about God.

Preliminary possibilities

I understand their perplexities. I would like to be able to say something useful to help, partly because more than once in my life I have faced this difficulty. Looking back at these experiences, I ask myself what I can say.

First of all, we must remain honest and not by-pass intellectual issues. Integrity must not be compromised. Even if in the past man's intellectual powers and motivations have been overestimated at the expense of his other gifts, we ought not now, I think, to swing with the pendulum to the other extreme and underestimate the value of reasoning. To do this would be to treat man as less than human.

13

The enquirer may not always be able to tackle these problems alone; he may well need someone to help him to work through them. He may find he has as much to unlearn as to discover. Perhaps some of his old ideas about prayer, faith and God he may find to be so inadequate as almost to be a parody of the truth. This preliminary period of seeking and searching may turn out to be surprisingly short; yet for others it may be a long process. We must all be ready for hard sustained effort.

My immediate concern is: what can I say to these men and women that will be of practical value about praying, while they are still engaged with these fundamental problems of God, of the universe and of individuals? Or, more bluntly, *until they are more sure about God, should their intellectual integrity compel them to keep off any kind of praying?* I do not think so. I am now very grateful that a priest encouraged me to go on with some sort of praying when as a student I was an agnostic. (Incidentally, we all know that Buddhists have forms of praying, although many of them have no interest in any creator-god or in theological questions. I am far from maintaining that Buddhist prayer is the same as Christian prayer, but there is some overlap between the two. This is specially clear from the writings of some Christian mystics.)

Then, next, two practical things. For me, both of these are close to prayer, though enquirers probably cannot see them in this light. First, I would encourage enquirers to go on meeting people, to try to understand them more deeply and to help them more effectively. There is a centuries-old Irish poem which says that we encounter the reality of God 'in mouth of friend and stranger', and that, I believe, is profoundly true, Secondly, I would recommend to them a way of reflecting on and exploring into life. This could be a kind of meditating which they might already be able to begin to practise without loss of intellectual integrity. Many people have discovered that, if they desire it, this way of simple reflection can gradually merge into some more defined experience of prayer, rather as the colours of the spectrum merge into one another. I intend to elaborate on these two suggestions in the next two chapters.

Wider understanding of prayer

Before doing this, I suggest that at least part of the trouble of those who find difficulty with prayer is that often they have tried to operate with too narrow an understanding of it. Lying behind that may well be too narrow a concept of God. We might even say, 'Your prayer has gone dead because your God is too small'. A first approximate definition of prayer might be a wide one: *prayer is an exploring of reality and a reflective engagement in life.* As we go on, we shall doubtless wish both to modify and to fill out this provisional description, but it will do for a start. (And if anyone should say that I had widened the meaning of prayer too much, I would remind him that the apostle Paul does the same thing with the word 'worship' in the twelfth chapter of the Letter to the Romans[3].)

Michael Novak, an American Catholic lay theologian and philosopher, also has said:

Prayer is penetrating through phantasy to reality and gathering courage to act.[4]

Einstein declared of all his scientific research, 'I am always seeking reality'. The same could be said of a historian as he attempts to find out how things exactly were and how they have since developed, or of a psychologist looking for truth about human personality, or of a sociologist searching for the truth about interactions in human society. All this seeking for truth is close to praying because, as Christian believers have always maintained, without the search for truth you cannot truly come to know God. It is only a small step beyond this to say that seeking truth is a kind of prayer, at least within this wider understanding of prayer. This step is even easier to make when we remember that, whatever else Christians may mean by the word God, they mean at least that reality which, hidden, underlies all phenomena, all happenings.

A number of groups of people spring to mind who, often without knowing it, are near to prayer – those who are engaged in the actual problems of life, in the sincere struggle for social and economic justice; those who work for true educational progress; those who fight against unjust racial, class and caste discrimination; those who labour in very varied ways for the health, physical, mental and spiritual, of mankind; and those who explore and try to meet the wide and deep needs of men and women, of young and old. All this generous and altruistic engagement in life is at least a beginning of being close to God, that is, a kind of prayer. This must be recognized at least by Christians, for they are deeply convinced that 'he who lives in love, lives in God' (1 John 4.16).

A word of caution is necessary here. Few things exasperate humanitarian agnostics or vague believers more than any implication that they, without knowing it, are already in some way men of prayer and almost believers. A Roman Catholic friend of mine, who has recently rejected all Christian belief, was very annoyed when a broad-minded priest said that my friend was still in spirit a Christian and a member of the church. Honesty demands that Christians should avoid any such apparently acquisitive terminology. Christians must not appear to claim that these men of goodwill somehow all belong to some kind of Christian party, some diffused church. But the only point I myself am trying to make here is that some men and women, who themselves are wishing to enter into the experience of Christian praying but are at present held back by intellectual difficulties, may not be as far off as they think they are.

Personal conviction

The further working out of the implications of what prayer might mean as exploration of reality and engagement in and reflection on life is the theme of the rest of this book.

16

But I think I should be less than honest if I did not, even at this point, anticipate and state the convictions to which I myself have been gradually led. Of course I realize that others may not share these convictions. I have not the slightest desire, as we go on with this enquiry, to evade facing up to other people's difficulties.

God, I now believe, dynamically interpenetrates the universe. That is, he is actively present in all persons and things though, of course, in very different degrees or modes. He is the spring of life, and he is what holds all things together in existence. Many people find it difficult, I know, to accept this, but the alternative seems to me to be sheer materialism, that is to say that basically matter alone is real. Neither of these two alternative interpretations of the universe, I grant, can be proved. In my opinion, we ultimately have to choose between them. In the end, our life style will show which we have chosen. For me, of these two alternatives, the dynamic divine interpenetration of the universe seems to raise fewer difficulties than materialism. I run the risk of over-simplification, but it seems to me that if we accept sheer materialism we take all depth out of aesthetic experience. For example, an evening's music would then be only the setting in motion of sound waves and the corresponding vibration in our eardrums, and that would be all. In the same way, all depth of meaning would, I think, be taken out of our most treasured personal relationships. For lovers the deepest and most understanding making of love would then be reduced to physical and chemical changes in the human body, and that would be all there was to it.

There is great difficulty in the accepting of this divine interpenetration of all things. If the divine is in everyone and everything, why is there evil and where has it come from? Something seems to have gone wrong with the universe. How it has happened I do not know. I do not expect a complete intellectual explanation of it. For even in the exact physical sciences we have to carry on with unresolved problems; in the study of light, so I understand, you have to hold side by side two apparently different hypotheses. On the one hand, light is understood as wave motion and, on the other hand, light is understood as *quanta*, pellets of energy. This apparent conflict does not lead the physicist to give up his physics and take to writing poetry instead! So the grave problem of evil and similar difficulties do not make the believer throw in his hand. Faced with the brute problem of evil, I feel that I am responsible for coping with it and fighting it, not solving it. Intellectually, the alternatives seem either to believe in God and accept the problem of evil, or else to reject any belief in God and to try to find some explanation for the beauty and goodness in the world. Of these two alternatives I myself find the former far less difficult.

This, all too briefly, is why I believe in the divine dynamic interpenetration of the universe. From such belief a conclusion follows. As we explore reality and engage in life and reflect upon it, we are there and then in direct touch with the divine. This is what we mean by God in his immanence, or, as we might say, that aspect of the divine which in varied ways runs through the universe. So, unknown to many, God *incognito* is meeting them in their persevering search, service and reflection. One day they may become *aware* of the divine who has been always with them. This is parallel to the way personal relationships often develop. You may be with a group of people, studying together, working together, sharing some interest or hobby, taking your pleasures together. Then one day you realize gradually or suddenly that your relationship with a particular person has become more personal. You had been with this person, but now in a deep sense you are *aware* of this person.

Let us follow up this parallel. This kind of human relationship may grow further into a rich friendship or it may even lead on to a deep, satisfying marriage. You then become more and more aware of one another and of one another's gifts and capacities. But even as your relationship matures far more deeply, you realize that there is a richness in your friend or partner beyond all that you know and experience. He transcends all the wonder of your friendship and love. So it is with our relationship with God. It is already wonderful to be aware of God's dynamic immanence in our search for reality and in our engagement in service. But something even more wonderful comes when we realize that God is far, far more than can be experienced in the way we have begun to know him. He transcends the relationship of immanence. He is *above* (not, of course, in any spatial sense) as well as *in* all relationships.

This is a disclosure we receive. We know him now not only as the 'One in whom we live and move and have our being' (Acts 17.27), but also as our Master and – may we not say so ? – as Love. We can neither argue ourselves into these disclosures nor seize them for ourselves. Simone Weil, a talented, left-wing Jewess, an unbeliever, came finally to a deep understanding of God through prayer. She wrote out of her own experience:

> They do not turn to God. How could they do so when they are in total darkness? God himself set their faces in the right direction. He does not, however, show himself to them for a long time. It is for them to remain motionless, and waiting, they know not for what.[5]

Sometimes it is rather like that at the beginning of deep friendship and profound human love; we need to be open and ready, but then we can only wait and receive.

But when we begin to receive, we must be prepared to act, to be changed and to continue to be changed. The result of accepting this reality has been well expressed by Peter Baelz, the Dean of Jesus College, Cambridge:

> The acknowledgement of the reality of the transcendent God is like seeing something to which I had previously been blind. It is like hearing something to which I had previously been deaf. But the seeing and the hearing are aspects of an event which affect my whole being as a person. It is not possible to remain unconcerned; I must act. And unless I deliberately reject what I see and hear, I

19

find myself responding to that which is revealed to me. My response is mine, and consequently it is free; nevertheless it is a response which is evoked from me and comes to me 'out of the blue'. I recognize it as a gift of grace, and not as an achievement of my own.[6]

For myself and for most Christians our understanding of the transcendence of God is linked very closely with the person of Jesus Christ. I shall have to write very much more about him because for me he is beginning to be so central to my living and praying. The apostle Paul wrote to his friends, 'To me to live is Christ' (Phil. 1.21). I must now briefly say three things about Jesus Christ; I will give my reasons later on. First, after trying to weigh the historical evidence, I am convinced that we have in the New Testament a sufficiently reliable picture of Jesus and of the impact he made on the first Christian communities. Secondly, we can see in him some quite basic factors of what being truly human will always involve – in many ways he is man *par excellence*. Thirdly, I am sure that through him there comes to us a disclosure of the character of the divine, immanent and transcendent, which is at the heart of reality. As Professor John Hick, another writer in this series, has put it, Jesus is 'God's attitude to mankind made flesh'.[7] Without Jesus God would be for me largely a hidden God. In Jesus I begin to see the divine translated into a human life and inviting me to respond in my living and praying. But for many people their discovery of Jesus is not only in the documents of the New Testament, it is in their experience of fellowship in a group of Christian friends. It is there they encounter the Spirit of Jesus. These groups are the cells of the living body of the church. They are of supreme importance.

We all have to find our own way to praying. But we are not alone. We can learn from what others have found and are finding in their search. We have to grasp for ourselves the coming to us of God in the balance of his immanence and transcendence. I cannot help regretting that so much traditional religious teaching has so over-emphasized the

20

transcendence of God at the cost of his immanence that God has too often been depicted almost as if he were the 'Big Boss'.

Many are looking for some kind of praying today. Without knowing it they are in contact with God *incognito* as they go on in their search, their service and their reflection. They may soon become *aware* of his immanence in the universe and in life. Then, through their experience of his immanence a sense of the divine transcendence may break through to them. There is no one path mapped out for everyone.

Dag Hammarskjöld of Sweden was in many ways a typical modern man. He was Secretary-General of the United Nations until his death in a plane crash, while he was trying to bring peace to the Congo. He had been brought up as a Christian in the Lutheran tradition. As a student he found his faith being eaten away by the acids of modernity. But he went on seeking. He kept a journal, *Markings*. There, in the middle of his committed life of service, he wrote one night:

> But at some moment I did answer *Yes* to Someone – or Something – and from that hour I was certain that existence is meaningful and that, therefore, my life in self-surrender had a goal.

NOTES

1. Pierre Teilhard de Chardin, *Le Milieu Divin*, London: Fontana 1964, and New York: Harper Torchbooks, p. 13. These editions have a sensitive introduction to his life by Pierre Leroy, SJ. This paperback, in spite of its French title, is a *translation* of a very original book. See also Pierre Teilhard de Chardin, *Letters from a Traveller*, London: Collins, and New York: Harper and Row 1962; *Letters to Léontine Zanta*, London: Collins 1969, and New York: Harper and Row 1968.

2. For an account of Charles de Foucauld and the Little Brothers, and of the principles of their life, see R. Voillaume, *Seeds of the Desert*, London: Burns and Oates, and Chicago: Fides 1955.

3. Romans 12.1. In the Greek version of the Old Testament, *latreia* (here translated as 'worship' or 'service') occurs nine times; it always refers to worship, except in II Macc. 4.14, where it is used of forced

labour. In the New Testament it occurs five times: in Rom. 9.4: Heb. 9.1, 6 it means worship: in John 16.2 the context shows it is equivalent to a sacrifice: there remains only our citation from Rom. 12.1. See 'Worship and Everyday Life, A Note on Romans 12', in E. Käsemann, *New Testament Questions of Today*, London: SCM Press, and Philadelphia: Fortress Press 1969, and particularly his conclusion: 'For the first time in the history of the Church the total activity of the community and its members is being looked at from a unified perspective' (p. 195).

4. M. Novak, *A Time to Build*, New York: Macmillan 1967, p. 283.

5. Simone Weil, *Waiting for God*, London: Routledge and Kegan Paul 1951, and New York: Capricorn 1959, p. 211.

6. P. R. Baelz, *Prayer and Providence*, London: SCM Press, and New York: Seabury Press 1968, pp. 27 f.

7. John Hick, *Christianity at the Centre*, London: SCM Press 1968, p. 38.

8. Dag Hammarskjöld, *Markings*, London: Faber 1964, and New York: Knopf 1965, p. 205. See also H. P. Van Dusen, *Dag Hammarskjöld: A Biographical Interpretation of 'Markings'*, London: Faber, and New York: Harper and Row 1967 (American title: *Dag Hammarskjöld: The Man and His Faith*).

2 Working is Praying

Laborare est orare

There are plenty of people nowadays, as we have seen, who wish somehow to pray, even while they are not sure of God. I have already suggested two things they might do, which may be very close to prayer, even before they have in any sense resolved the God-question for themselves. These are the subjects of this and the following chapter. The first will be a way of truly meeting and serving our neighbour; this may be in our everyday work or in the true care of our family, as well as in the many modern forms of service. The second subject, the theme of chapter 3, will be some kind of fairly systematic reflection on life.

In the Assembly of the World Council of Churches at Uppsala I listened attentively to the debate on worship and prayer in plenary session. At the end it was decided to insert into the Assembly's report the following words:

> We believe that in the service of their neighbour, men can meet the Lord, to whom the community of faith looks in prayer, that that community is open to and supports the perplexed, and that the desire to pray is the groping of doubt into faith.[1]

Every phrase in that sentence makes a point. In particular the Assembly endorsed that serving one's neighbour is meeting the Lord and therefore presumably is a form of praying.

This widening of the common idea of prayer is not a new idea as some people might think. Medieval Christians put it in a Latin tag, *Laborare est orare* – to work is to pray –

23

though perhaps they might have been wiser to say *Laborare sit orare* – to work may be to pray. Earlier still there are hints of this wider understanding of prayer in the Bible itself. Ben Sira, in one of the books of the Apocrypha, said about the craftsmen and workmen of the city:

> They keep stable the fabric of the world
> And their prayer is in the practice of their trade   (Sirach 38.34)

In the same sort of way, Jeremiah the prophet spoke with approval of King Josiah:

> He judged the cause of the poor and needy;
>   then it was well.
> Is not this to know me?
>   says the Lord   (Jer. 22.16)

It is significant that the prophet did not say that judging the poor and needy was a result of knowing God through prayer, but rather that judging the poor and needy was in itself a knowing of the Lord. Again, there is the saying in the gospel parable, 'I was in prison and you came to me' (Matt. 25.36). Because knowing the Lord and coming to the Lord are very much what we mean by prayer, it follows that those who are doing justice and service are in some sort of way praying. They may, in the wider sense which we have given to prayer, be beginning to pray without realizing it themselves. It is to the point to notice this about the parable. The man who visited the prison did not recognize in the person of the prisoner the Lord himself, still less did he have faith in the Lord.

It might be best for those who are unsure of God and yet somehow wish to pray to go on by continuing in their service with vigour and hope, but also looking *beyond the present horizons of their serving*. We must, of course, acknowledge at once that some agnostics and atheists are more generous and effective in their service than some believers. I do not wish to minimize this in the slightest degree. Yet I am convinced that we all need to look beyond the present horizons of our service in four ways: considering the total needs of those whom we try to serve; realizing the necessity of some degree of disinvolvement in the middle of our engagement in service; finding resilience in our service and having our motives purified as well as strengthened. In each of these ways we may find ourselves led beyond where we now are and towards a deeper idea of prayer.

Total needs

But before we can consider these four matters, we must straightaway remove an obvious misunderstanding. We must not, of course, be self-conscious in meeting and serving others, still less paternalistic. In fact, we often receive more than we give. For example, those who work amongst the sick and aged are sometimes inspired by the courage of their patients and by their deep concern for other people. It may be a platitude, but it needs to be repeated again and again, that in all contact with others, everyone needs to guard against an insidious sense of superiority. We need to learn how to receive from others, as well as to give to them.

It is the total needs of others that we should try to consider. We may find ourselves forced to attend to one particular need of a person; this may be due to the urgency of that need, or to the pressure of time, or to our own particular qualifications. Yet we should prefer not to deal with only one symptom of need, but rather to see the person as man, woman or child in his full setting and needs. Man's total needs include his basic physical needs, his education for life, his personal relationships and, I would add, his growing relationship with that great Reality whom we speak of as God. These four kinds of needs cannot be sharply divided from one another, and we must look in turn at each of them in this enquiry into a wider understanding of prayer.

First, we shall rightly and naturally be concerned with the crying needs for adequate food, shelter and medical care. No one who has seen men sleeping on the pavements of

Bombay can forget this basic demand in India and in many areas of undeveloped countries; nor can anyone turn a blind eye on these basic needs who has seen the worst of the black ghettoes in the United States, or the grimmer areas surviving in most of the rich countries of the west. Here involvement itself borders on prayer. 'When I was hungry, you gave me food; when I was a stranger, you took me into your home' (Matt. 25.35 NEB). Nor should we, as in the past missionaries and Christian philanthropists have sometimes done, use this service as mere bait to 'raise people's minds to higher things'. According to the gospels, Jesus often healed men's bodies and let them go; seldom did he use physical healing as a lever to make them concerned about their 'spiritual state'. The World Council of Churches' Assembly at Uppsala in its report on Mission stated:

> We Christians know that we are in this worldwide struggle for meaning, dignity, freedom and love, and we cannot stand aloof. We have been charged with a message and a ministry that have to do with more than material needs, but we can never be content to treat our concern for physical and social needs as merely secondary to our responsibility for the needs of the spirit.[2]

In New Testament times Christians were in no position to put political or social pressure on the government to meet these fundamental needs of the people of their day. Our situation is quite different. Such actions now by believers and men of goodwill may form an integral expression of *living* prayer.

Secondly, modern medicine and psychiatry have underlined what we have long known, that we cannot separate health of body and health of mind: *mens sana in corpore sano*. This therefore involves some kind of reform in education – and without undue delay. There is overwhelming evidence that hidden abilities, intellectual and artistic, are allowed to run to waste; these must be discovered and developed for the good of all. Nor should young men and women be groomed to run a ruthless and unjust competitive or oppressive society. Many students and far-sighted people are now determined about this. But what precise changes should be made in different countries and situations? Reflection, personal and corporate, on all these matters is part of the exploration of and engagement in life which we have described as prayer; and so is also the shaking and waking up of the more dormant powers-that-be. Education has never ended with leaving school or going down from the university. Still less does it end there in these days of television, transistors, expanding journalism and of paperbacks. The World Council of Churches' Report on the Joint Study Commission on Education stated to the Uppsala Assembly:

> Education has broken out of the schoolroom. Out-of-school education, as it is called, enlists now millions of adults everywhere. Universities and colleges develop extension programmes that bring systematic instruction to communities far from the campuses; municipal agencies support specialized classes.
>
> And out-reaching, out-racing them all are the mass media – radio, television, the press, cinema, records, popular culture's common carriers pressing on the whole population their random, incessant education. Some of it is by intent and design education, even superb education, in the most classic sense of the word. But all of it, good, bad and indifferent, is educational, accomplishing at its own high pitch and furious tempo just what all the rest of the out-of-school programmes do in their own way. Much is now being learned by many where the school is nowhere in sight. In fact, the largest education of all involves most of the population most of the time. Everywhere and always the voices and happenings and pressures of our churning history work their incessant instructions: providing new information, testing old 'facts', flexing taken-for-granteds, getting men ready whether they want to be readied or not for the personal, social, political, technical novelties so tumultuously breaking in on us whether we are ready or not.[3]

Our reflective discussion and discrimination on these matters, our protest and appreciation, form part of this wider understanding of prayer. None of us can do all this. The world of knowledge and action is now far too wide. We can no longer breed the many-sided Renaissance man. This is not to say that we should not stretch our powers.

But in our desire to serve we can spread ourselves too thinly. We must recognize our own limitations; we must complement one another's abilities. This makes it clear that prayer and worship in the sense of reflection and engagement in life needs to a great extent to be corporate.

Thirdly, this brings us to the question of personal relationships. Whatever changes we may be able to make for people's health, living conditions and education in its broadest sense, the benefit of these improvements will be greatly reduced unless their personal relationships are at least tolerably good. These relationships cannot be satisfactory until people feel that they are being completely accepted by others as fellow human beings. It is not enough that they should be treated in this way; they need to feel that this is so. Where they do not feel it, there is fuel for great bitterness.

We know what it is to treat people as cases, as numbers and as mere cogs in a business or in an administrative machine. But it is not easy to put precisely into words what it means to be accepted completely as a person, though we all sense for ourselves the difference between being treated personally and less than personally. Unfortunately not everyone seems able to help others to feel that they are being accepted fully as fellow human beings; and how to convey this to others cannot be learned from books and study alone. Perhaps we can only share it after we ourselves have felt truly accepted by other people. This is something which cannot be known merely through the normal give-and-take of ordinary life, but rather which comes to us from particular relationships with some few men and women who truly love and care for us as persons. This often comes through our own experience of family life, of friendship and love, and sometimes through sharing in a small Christian or other informal group. These small groups, as I will try to show later, may also be an important way of discovering the reality of prayer. Nearly all people could, I think, find them helpful, but perhaps specially those who for some reason find it difficult to convey to others the feeling that they are accepting them completely as persons.

We may all learn how we may do this more deeply by watching others do it and also by reading the biographies and personal writings of those thousands who have had a notable gift for this. We see it in Father Damien sharing the daily life of lepers at Kakaako in the Pacific until one Sunday morning he began his sermon with words literally true, 'We lepers . . .'.[4] We find it, less dramatically, in Forbes Robinson, living as a chaplain of a Cambridge college: to him no one was 'a mere student, one of a mass'; he made the most ordinary person feel for himself that 'his own life, however commonplace with all its failures and inconsistencies, was a tremendous enterprise, big with opportunities'. It is amazing the influence this man had, in spite of chronic ill-health before he died at thirty-seven; and, incidentally, one who knew him intimately said, 'Prayer was to him the very breath of life'.[5]

It is widely agreed that Jesus was very gifted in this discerning of people's real needs and in helping them to feel that they were fully accepted as persons. He first let them see that he identified himself with them. In contrast to the sincere but more standard type of religious man, John the Baptist, they said about Jesus, 'Look at him! a glutton and a drinker' (Luke 7.34 NEB). Without condoning their faults, he accepted them as they were and helped them to realize their own potentialities, sometimes using unexpected methods. He cut straight through conventional ways to help a woman when she had been caught in the very act of adultery. He also uncovered and developed the best in Peter, beneath his surface impulsiveness and cowardice, and trained him for responsibility and leadership. Jesus was ready to use even some degree of violence in the temple itself when the 'establishment' was hindering people from receiving the help they needed and should have received there. It is important to take time frequently to reflect on these things and, I would add, on the undoubted fact that

Jesus' relation with people was inextricably interwoven with his own strong sense of dependence on God. What do we make of his times of solitude in a garden or on a mountain-side, at dawn or in the silence of the night? Is this man as man might be in the fullness of human nature?

Fourthly, this raises another question: has man a further need besides his physical, intellectual and cultural needs, and besides his need for interpersonal relationships? In order to realize his full potentialities as man, does man need some conscious relation with a Reality wider than his family and fellow-men? We all know admirable, integrated people, who are unbelievers; but this does not entirely answer the question about man's total potentialities. Many people are unaware of all kinds of unrealized potentialities. Nicolas Berdyaev, who was near enough to Marxism to be appointed to a chair of philosophy at Moscow University after the Russian revolution but who later returned to the Orthodox church of his birth, wrote significantly towards the end of a lifetime of varied experience, 'Man without God is no longer man'.[6] By this he meant, I presume, that man to be fully man needs not only human relationships but also some kind of conscious relationship with God. What if man to be alive with his whole being needs to be able to make authentically his own the words of the Jewish poet:

> Like as the hart desireth the water-brooks,
> So longeth my soul after thee, O God,
>> My soul is athirst for God,
>> Yea, for the living God?

This desire for God, that is, for Reality which is not only within ourselves but is also beyond ourselves, has, I grant, sometimes expressed itself in unbalanced ways. But the desire for human love has also often expressed itself in strange, unbalanced ways. These facts do not seem to me to invalidate either our longing for human love or our desire for the divine Reality. In fact, there is considerable evidence to show that human love and the desire for the divine can enrich and shed light on one another. A very perceptive writer on living and praying, Hans Urs von Balthasar, chaplain to the Roman Catholic students at Basel University, has given it as his tested conviction, 'The created person who is loved is grasped in his true reality only in relation to God'.[7]

Engagement and disinvolvement

To consider these elements in the total needs of men and women demands some leisure for reflection. When I see many people so incessantly involved in their daily work, in their care for their families and in many forms of voluntary service, I feel concerned about them. I am anxious for them – and not only for them but also for those whom they are trying to help. I cannot help wondering whether in this ceaseless demand on their physical and nervous resources they can keep a true sense of proportion. Is it possible that they might be more truly and effectively involved if they had, under normal circumstances, times of disinvolvement? It was Albert Camus, the French existentialist, who maintained:

> To understand the world, it is necessary sometimes to turn away from the world; to serve men better, it is necessary for a moment to keep them at a distance.[8]

The historian Arnold Toynbee's encyclopaedic study led him to the conclusion that only through some measure of disengagement can a person's full capacities be released and put to the service of his neighbour:

> The disengagement and withdrawal make it possible for the personality to realize individual potentialities which might have remained in abeyance if the individual in whom they were immanent had not been released for a moment from his social toils and trammels.[9]

This is emphasized in an article on 'Prayer and Worldly Holiness':

> We can and must 'go apart' at times, for such moments of withdrawal are a time of taking stock, of sharpening one's perspective, of penetrating more deeply into the awesomeness of reality itself.

31

We need to sit down at times to ponder, to wonder, to get in touch with and to keep open to the mystery of God and of man's relationship to him and to his fellow men. The moment of prayer is necessary if one is to be fully and humanly present to one's fellow men when the time for such encounter arrives. Such meditative moments are a constant reassessing of the value of human things, a continual reminder of oneself and a deepening of one's appreciation for the contacts with one's neighbour and with the world, which will ensue that day. . . . Withdrawing for reflection is necessary for getting hold of oneself, for gathering one's forces. We need to stand back at times to get a broader view, lest our own little particular loves, our own secure little corners of the world blur our cosmic vision.[10]

Resilience

Another thing which troubles me is when I see people in their generosity working so incessantly that they lose not only their sense of proportion but also their vitality. They work longer and longer, but slower and slower. They lose their resilience, especially as they come to see that in their struggles for justice and brotherhood they are up against more human inertia, human guile and human perversity. History appears to show that something more evil than men's conscious powers can sweep through a nation; one instance of this was the Nazis' attempt at a wholesale obliteration of the Jews. The New Testament speaks of our struggle against these evil forces as a 'fight not against human foes but against cosmic powers, against the authorities and potentates of this dark world, against the superhuman forces of evil' (Eph. 6.12 NEB). This is the picture language of mythology, but it stands for some forces of impersonal evil which somehow break out from the individual and corporate subconscious of whole peoples. If the evil we have to contend with were only perverse human ingenuity, our conscious resolute human efforts might be enough. But if it is more than this, then we need to see whether it is in any way possible to open ourselves to a source of good commensurate with this deep-seated evil. This, I suggest, is something which all men of goodwill might consider investigating. We have already given as a preliminary description of prayer the exploration of reality as well as engagement in life. With this exploration of the deep good, which we have reason to believe is at the heart of reality, we are less likely to be gradually worn down by the forces of evil. In fact, we may in this way discover the secret of resilience.

Purification of motives

The fourth way in which we might look beyond the horizons of our service is to recognize that we need to have our motivation not only strengthened but also progressively purified from egoism. We should obviously enjoy meeting and helping others, and it is clearly good and right to experience some sense of fulfilment in this way. In fact, to enjoy what we are doing often means that we are doing it well, and it is certainly a useful incentive, particularly for the beginner. Yet we all need to be kept alert to the fact of how easily and subtly our meeting and serving others can be spoilt by a touch of patronage or a sense of superiority. During the last century in Britain and in other countries the under-privileged often either writhed under the well-meaning paternalism of their 'betters' or else had their justifiable discontent smothered by it. It has been far more serious in Asia and Africa. Resentment has built up on a vast scale among the new nations against their former rulers and benefactors from the west. The service they gave was often genuine enough and sometimes sacrificial, yet again and again it was marred by an irritatingly condescending and paternalistic manner. Asians and Africans were seldom accepted fully as fellow human beings. It is understandable how it happened. It was the almost inevitable outcome of that pride and self-centredness which we find so subtly and so deeply rooted in all human nature. Experience further shows that we cannot ourselves eliminate pride and egoism. In fact, if we attempt to do this self-consiously and systematically by our own efforts, the result may well be that we only become proud of the fact that we are not quite as proud as we used to be! We seem to be caught in a vicious circle of pride.

But there are times when we begin to lose our pre-occupation with ourselves, our failures, our successes, our reputations; and we find ourselves unselfconsciously looking away from ourselves to God, the great Reality, who is not only in all things, but is over all things. This unselfconscious looking away from ourselves to God is often carried over with an authentic humility into all our service and daily relationships. This is what prayer and worship really should be. Yet honesty compels us to admit that some, who are regular in formal worship, are often self-complacent and self-centred, while some unbelievers are admirably unselfconscious in their service. Even so there is a considerable amount of evidence to show that genuine worship 'disinfects our service from egoism'.[11]

NOTES

1. *Uppsala Report*, Geneva: WCC 1968, p. 78.

2. *Ibid.*, p. 28.

3. *Work Book* for the Uppsala Assembly Committee, Geneva: WCC 1968, pp. 167 f.

4. J. Farrow, *Damien the Leper*, New York: Doubleday 1957, p. 160.

5. Forbes Robinson, *Letters to His Friends*, London: Longmans 1909: quotation from an appreciation by D. B. Kittermaster, pp. 42–53. There is a later edition, M. R. J. Manktelow, *Forbes Robinson: Disciple of Love*, London: S.P.C.K. 1961, pp. 11–14.

6. N. Berdyaev, *The End of Our Time*, London: Sheed and Ward 1935, p. 54.

7. Hans Urs von Balthasar, *Science, Religion and Christianity*, London: Burns and Oates 1958, and New York: Seabury Press 1967 (American title: *The God-question and Modern Man*), p. 147.

8. Albert Camus, *L'été*, Paris: Gallimard 1954, p. 13.

9. A. J. Toynbee, *A Study of History*, vol. III, London: Oxford University Press 1956, p. 248.

10. G. M. Schutte, SSpS, 'Reflections on Prayer and Worldly Holiness', *Worship*, February 1967, p. 110.

11. H. Bremond, *Literary History of Religious Thought in France*, London: S.P.C.K. 1928. This is the beginning of the translation of his captivating work in eleven volumes, *Histoire Littéraire du Sentiment Religieux en France*, Paris Bloud et Gay 1928, vol. vii, p. 15.

3 Reflecting is Praying

Not beginning with God

When people wish to pray, even if they are uncertain about God, there are at least two ways they can set about it. One way is the way of service as we saw in the last chapter. Another way is reflecting on life, and this eventually may merge into that kind of explicit prayer which grasps the reality of God, transcendent as well as immanent, and expresses to him our concern for our neighbours and for the world. But we can start with straightforward reflection on life without bringing in explicitly religious ideas. To many people nowadays traditional religious talk sounds phoney. Their reflecting must start with what seems real and authentic to them. That is why they cannot begin with God or at least with God in the way many people have thought about him in the past. It would be better for them to begin by reflecting on their own experience. Some people would not call this praying. But if we take our broad description of prayer as exploration of reality and reflective engagement in life, then this reflecting itself, if it is sincere, may be called a kind of prayer. Perhaps this is what was meant by that sensitive and orthodox theologian, Dr Austin Farrer, when at the beginning of his Bampton Lectures in Oxford he spoke of his own experience of prayer as a young man:

> I thought of myself as set over against the deity as one man faces another across a table, except that God was invisible and infinitely great. And I hoped that he might signify his presence to me by way of colloquy, but neither out of the scripture I read nor in the prayers I tried to make did any mental voice address me. So I would no

longer attempt, with the psalmist, 'to set God before my face'. I would see him as *the underlying cause of my thinking*, especially of those thoughts in which I tried to think of him. I would dare to think that sometimes my thought would become diaphanous, so that there might be some perception of the divine cause shining through the created effect, as a deep pool, settling into a clear tranquillity, permits me to see the spring in the bottom of it from which its waters rise. I would dare to hope that through a second cause the First Cause might be felt, when the second cause in question was itself a spirit, made in the image of the Divine Spirit, and perpetually welling up out of his creative act.[1]

Of course an agnostic would not wish to speak like this of his own reflections, yet believers could in the light of faith see even an unbeliever's reflections in this way, for as von Balthasar says:

We have to recall that God, the sea and abyss of Being, is not a being among others, hence not an 'object' that might be detached from a surrounding world and especially not from the knowing subject.[2]

In the past people were often advised to reflect on their own needs and weaknesses. It was claimed that this might well bring them to a sense of God and of his power to help them. This sometimes has been undeniably effective. But to try to induce artificially in yourself or in others a sense of need as a step towards faith in God is often, I think, an unwise procedure. Experience shows that this sometimes leads to unfortunate reactions. In general it is better nowadays to begin with reflections on experiences of wonder, joy, relief and gratitude rather than those of need or weakness, particularly because many modern people suspect that religion is a 'snuffing around in the sins of men in order to catch them out', as Dietrich Bonhoeffer put it in one of his letters from a Nazi prison; and because it is important, as he also wrote, to make it clear at once that:

We should frankly recognize that the world, and people have come of age, that we should not run down man in his worldliness, but confront him with God at his strongest point.[3]

36

Gratitude spontaneous and reflective

We ought to express our gratitude much more spontaneously in the normal run of life. At moments of thankfulness, of relief, of exhilaration, of achievement, it is good to exclaim on the spur of the moment 'Thanks be to God', though we may be quite vague about God, or even just to say 'Thanks be'. If prayer is the exploration of reality, then as explorers we must begin by loosening up our muscles, and this is one way of doing it.

Expressing gratitude and relief also to friends more freely and spontaneously would have a similar useful result. Less stiff upper lip, and less 'Not so bad, thank you'. Of course we must be natural about it and take into account our own and our friends' temperaments. Then these words of thankfulness would not only express but also deepen our sense of mutual interdependence on one another, and in time these words might also lead to a healthy sense of dependence on that great underlying reality, whom believers call God. Dr Harry Guntrip, a psychiatrist, maintains that this sense of dependence is essential both for human maturity and also for the life of faith, and that these two strengthen one another:

> Dependence is, in fact, an ineradicable element in human nature, and the whole development of love and affection arises out of our need for one another. From this point of view religion is concerned with the basic fact of personal relationship and man's quest for a radical solution to the problems that arise out of his dependent nature.[4]

Yet besides these spontaneous expressions of thankfulness we need also to set aside times for reflective gratitude. We should then try to find some kind of linking between these experiences. It is in this kind of way that personal relationships are often deepened; for example, when someone receives a present or a kindness from a friend, he often asks himself how his friend came to know that he would like this, and so he reflects with gratitude over earlier meetings and conversations. A similar interrelating of our grateful

37

reflections on life may weave a kind of tapestry of thankfulness and so deepen our confidence in life and give us the desire and the courage to explore it.

We should naturally think with gratitude of our friends and of those who are specially close to us. But it would be a good thing also to include appreciative reflection about other people, particularly those whose abilities and achievements might make us envious or those against whom we might bear resentment. Reflection then might make us more realistic about ourselves and more free from jealousy and animosity. In this way our whole exploration of life would be more objective and discerning. This is the kind of reflective gratitude we find in the great men of faith and of prayer. The apostle Paul wrote to his friends at Philippi, 'I thank my God whenever I think of you' (Phil. 1.3 NEB); and even to the church at Corinth, though it was corrupted by rivalries and scandals, he could say, 'I am always thanking God for you. I thank him for his grace given to you in Christ Jesus. I thank him for all the enrichment that has come to you in Christ' (1 Cor. 1.4–5a). He was not turning a blind eye to their faults or, as has sometimes been said, trying to win their support by flattering them. Rather, he was discerning and reflecting upon the signs of goodness beneath the unattractive exterior of this Christian community. It is worth noticing as well that Paul's thankfulness expressed itself in his devoting himself to the service of others; and it is in this sequence that he is led to pray for them – gratitude, devotion to their service, prayer.

Reflective gratitude must surely in our age include thankfulness for the benefits of science, medicine and technology. What difference they make to life can perhaps only be appreciated by those who have lived in very underdeveloped countries. Most of us in the west take these benefits too much for granted with hardly any sense of thankfulness. Incidentally, this part of reflective gratitude might also do something to remove the lurking groundless fear which some people have that science is somehow inimical to faith and prayer. If there is a danger to be guarded against in this age of technology and development, it is perhaps that technologists may develop a dominating frame of mind, because in their daily work they may, as it were, have to stand over nature and seize and apply its resources and energies for their own purposes and, we hope, for the good of humanity. But a dominating outlook, however acquired, is neither good for personal relationships nor for the life of faith and prayer.

This is why we need to express our gratitude also for the arts, and we can see the counterbalancing effect of a deep and grateful appreciation of literature and poetry. The lover of literature in contrast to the technologist must sit beneath the given text and let it speak to him. He needs to read with docility, not with a childish docility, but with an 'informed docility' arising from his past experience and study. In the building up of good personal relationships also such 'informed docility' drawing on the past and being ready to be led forward into the future is clearly an asset. The same is true in that exploration of life, which is prayer.

Grateful appreciation of poetry is important for a further reason. Many of those, who have tried through prayer to explore the reality of life, have left us the records of their experience in poetry. The heart of what they have come to know has been, as we say, 'too deep for words', like some experiences of friendship and human love. For them the descriptive words of plain prose have been so inadequate. It has been poetry and illuminative imagery that they have had to use to convey to us what they have experienced. Two modern Benedictine monks show how they have been driven to poetry in their book on *The Experience of Prayer*. We read in the foreword:

Only the language of poetry is found adequate to articulate a man's consciousness at his most alive and aware, which is his prayer.[5]

The Christian Scriptures contain much of the experience of the pioneers of this search (as well as plenty of evidence of the conservative resistance of unimaginative self-centred human nature to this exploration). These Scriptures are to a far larger extent than the average man realizes a rich library of poetry and allusive imagery. That is why the typically post-Vatican II Catholic theologian, Karl Rahner, is justified in writing:

> The capacity and practice of perceiving the poetic word is a presupposition of hearing the Word of God. No doubt grace also creates this presupposition for itself, and no doubt there are many men whose ear and heart are open for the seminal poetry of eternal existence only in the Christian message itself. But this does not alter the basic truth that we have arrived at, that the poetic word and the poetic ear are so much part of man that if this essential power were really lost to the heart, man could no longer hear the Word of God in the word of man. In its inmost essence, the poetic is a prerequisite for Christianity.[6]

Wordsworth put this more bluntly over a century ago:

> This is a truth and an awful one, because to be incapable of a feeling of poetry, in my sense of the word, is to be without love of human nature and reverence for God.[7]

Art and music as well clearly play for countless people a major part in this discovery of the wealth and range of life, which prayer helps us to explore. It is significant how many of those who march and protest in the struggle for peace and social justice will also spend hours listening to music, whether classical music, or else modern and folk music. In their experience these things go together as part of their search for life and true 'humanness'.

The appreciation of the beauty and of the moods of nature as well, and above all the enrichment of life through companionship and love, can powerfully feed this reflective gratitude and lead towards this profound search into reality. If Wordsworth may be quoted again, he wrote a letter which, in spite of its quaint, archaic style, has curious similarity with the approach we are now suggesting:

> Theologians may puzzle their heads about dogmas as they will, the religion of gratitude cannot mislead us. Of that we are sure, and

gratitude is the handmaid to hope, and hope the harbinger of faith. I look abroad upon nature, I think of the best part of our species, I lean upon my friends and I meditate upon the Scriptures, especially the Gospel of St John; and my creed rises up of itself with the ease of an exhalation yet a fabric of adamant.[8]

To sum up, personally the more I reflect, the wider I find the range of my gratitude, and the more I desire to penetrate reality through prayer and to be involved in life.

But I must now guard myself against misunderstanding. This stress on reflective gratitude does not mean that we ignore the great evils of life, which will not fit into it – earthquakes and natural disasters, wars, persecutions, injustices and hatreds of men, to say nothing about torture and psychological manipulation in confinement camps, and about the threat of nuclear and biochemical warfare. We must not evade or minimize these problems with superficial answers. We know, of course, that in nearly all fields of reflection and study there are unresolved dilemmas, but this list is indeed formidable for believers. Also, in most individuals' experiences there are sufferings and frustrations. Sometimes people have brought these troubles upon themselves, there is no point in denying that; but there are plenty of other misfortunes for which they are not responsible. There these evils stand in the world and in individual lives as out of place as the geologists' erratic boulders, odd and not belonging to the landscape. Much more can be said about the problem of evil.[9] Our reflective gratitude must not make us blind to these evils, nor allow us to be crushed by them, nor to acquiesce in them, but rather to strengthen us to face their challenge, to cope with them, to battle through them. This reflection upon and exploration into life may lead us eventually to share in the insight of the apostle Paul, though he expressed it partly in terms strange to modern man:

In everything, as we know, he (the Spirit) co-operates for good with those who love God and are called according to his purpose. For I am convinced that there is nothing in death or life, in the realm of spirits or superhuman powers, in the world as it is or the world as it shall be, in the forces of the universe, in heights or depths – nothing in all creation that can separate us from the love of God in Christ Jesus our Lord (Rom. 8.28, 38–39 NEB).

This insight enabled him to cope with incessant responsibility, nerve-racking insecurities and appalling sufferings, and even more, to inspire others with his courage. The exploration of life through prayer may not explain evils, but it can strengthen us with other people to challenge them.

Material and method

To return now to reflective gratitude. This, like so many other things, needs to be fed and nourished. Discussion will help, but reading also will be important. I do not mean only religious reading. Useful material will come from many corners of life and often from unexpected ones. Some years ago my own attempts at praying were stimulated by two books about Edward Wilson, the ornithologist on Captain Scott's fatal journey to the South Pole, *Edward Wilson of the Antarctic* and *Edward Wilson: Nature-Lover*, containing reproductions of brilliant sketches he made at many degrees below zero.[10] The more directly religious literature is immense, indeed excessive. It is a question of finding some knowledgeable person to help us choose what will feed and give direction to our own reflections. On the whole it is better to read primary sources rather than rehashed accounts of other people's methods of meditation and prayer. Those who have made this search before us, men and women of most diverse types, have left us their own first-hand accounts, diaries, letters, prayers and writings. But much of it was written when the philosophical, religious and social outlooks were very different from our own, and in general when the understanding of human nature was inevitably less profound than it now is. Therefore this literature needs to be read with discrimination. Particularly valuable are writings which show a first-hand knowledge of the typical problems of modern men and women, such as Simone Weil, *Waiting for God*; Teilhard de Chardin, *Le Milieu Divin*; and Dag Hammarskjöld, *Markings*: and many have found the value of this last book doubled by reading Henry P. Van Dusen's *Dag Hammarskjöld*: *Christian Statesman*: *the Man and his Faith*, a biographical interpretation.

One of the books to nourish our reflections will naturally be the Bible. This is not, of course, one ponderous volume, but a library of books of very varied types. Some sections of it may be of use to us quite early in our search, such as, for instance, Paul's reflections on love in the thirteenth chapter of his First Letter to the Corinthians, or what the First Letter of John has to say on the question, still very much discussed, of the relation between love for our fellow-men and the love of God. But beginners and re-beginners will need a guide to this bewildering collection of books. We should be wise to take the advice of Baron von Hügel, an encyclopaedic scholar and man of prayer, who recommended us to be like the cows in the meadow, for they feed on the particular grass that suits them at the moment, and do not waste energy in snorting at the kind of grass they find inedible – and they also chew the cud.[11]

We had now better consider how best we can use these times of reflection. Vague, random thinking clearly will not do. On the other hand, there is no agreed standard method. Everyone must discover what is effective for himself, and everyone must be ready to change as time goes on. As in other parts of life we might find out what has helped other people and see if we can usefully adapt it to our own situation.

I will try to put one way of reflecting as simply as I can. It may even be too simple. I would suggest four steps. First, *stillness*. Some, as they put it, just 'unwind'; others would say that words like, 'Be still, and know that I am God', help them to begin. It helps me to start my praying if I picture mountains where I have enjoyed my holidays, or if I say to myself some words of the Bible which have come to mean a good deal to me, or if I remember Jesus as a man

43

whose life and character show us what is at the heart of reality. Other people will have other ways; but you cannot day-dream into reflection. Secondly, *purpose*. Some people recall the purpose and aims of their lives. I myself think of the divine purpose which I believe has been disclosed to us, and which is summarized for me in the words 'Thy Kingdom come on earth'. At this moment I also often remind myself of my own vocation. Thirdly, *reflection*. In the perspective of this purpose we reflect on whatever may naturally occur to us about the issues of the world, and about the happenings in our lives; we do this as far as we can in a positive and grateful way, as I suggested earlier in this chapter. Fourthly, after reflection, *commitment*. Reflection should lead to action: it may be something that we ought to do personally in the next twenty-four hours, a letter to be answered or a call to be made: it may be some joint action we ought to take on with others. If it is any major matter, we should be wise to check it with someone whose judgment we can trust.

About using words in these times of reflection. Those who are believers may address words to God. This must not be misunderstood. They are not so naïve as to think that their words give information to God or that words can persuade God to alter his mind. But they use words partly to give definiteness to their attitude of trust, as mature sons, in God as Father; and this is very important to them. Also they use words partly to express and identify their true selves, to be 'real', without pretence or façade. In these ways they make explicit their desire to co-operate in the divine purpose for others. I grant that Christians sometimes 'prattle' to God and in this way seem to attempt to persuade themselves that what they wish to do is definitely God's purpose for them. We can guard ourselves against such distortions. Silence and receptiveness matter. These times are better regarded as reflection than as dialogue.

Experience convinces me that these times often renew and refresh us in the pressure of life. They do this more effectively if we can set aside a short time regularly, if possible daily, for this reflection. Occasionally almost everyone fails through laziness to make the necessary effort. But it is not always through laziness; sometimes this reflection actually looks like a waste of time compared with some duty. The really urgent need of a neighbour must of course come first. But this meditative reflection should be a high priority, for it helps us to see life in the true perspective, to reassess our situation, to appreciate those we are going to meet, and to gather our energies to live resiliently. When days of abnormal pressure make this reflection practically impossible, the perspective and resilience it normally gives should carry us through these exceptional times.

There are days when nothing seems to happen. No new insight comes either on the issues and opportunities of our daily life or on the major problems of our society and the world. But then sometimes light dawns unexpectedly. Michael Polanyi, in his book *Personal Knowledge*, shows that even in natural science sudden illuminations come. We have known this at least since the time of Archimedes. It was at the moment that he was stepping into the bath that it flashed upon him how to test whether the king's crown was of gold or of an alloy, and he rushed out naked shouting, 'Heureka, heureka, I have found it, I have found it'. If we go on reflecting and seeking, we shall have our *heureka* moments. Light may come like a flash of lightning or gradually like the dawn of day. At such times it is fortunate if we have at hand some experienced friend who can interpret this new insight and can help us to work out its implications.

It is always helpful, and especially at these times, to have a small group of friends we know well and can talk to freely (I speak from experience), some of whom have some real understanding of prayer, and some of whom are little more than beginners and seekers, though probably none of them would classify themselves in these ways. It was out of such a group that there came two of the most unpretentious

45

and unconventional books which have stimulated and helped a very wide range of people, *Prayers of Life* and *The Christian Response*.[12] We will turn to such groups in the next chapter.

NOTES

1. A. M. Farrer, *The Glass of Vision*, London: Dacre Press 1948, pp. 7 f. (italics mine).

2. Hans Urs von Balthasar, *Science, Religion and Christianity*, p. 147.

3. Dietrich Bonhoeffer, *Letters and Papers from Prison*, London: SCM Press, and New York: The Macmillan Company 1967, pp. 192 f.

4. H. Guntrip, quoted in E. James (ed.), *Spirituality for Today*, London: SCM Press 1968, p. 33.

5. S. Moore and K. Maguire, *The Experience of Prayer*, London: Darton, Longman and Todd 1969, p. 8.

6. Karl Rahner SJ, 'Poetry and the Christian', in *Theological Investigations IV*, London: Darton, Longman and Todd, and Baltimore: Helicon Press 1966, p. 363.

7. William Wordsworth, quoted in W. R. Inge, *Studies of English Mystics*, London: Murray 1900, p. 189.

8. M. Moorman, *William Wordsworth*, Vol. II, London: Oxford University Press 1965, pp. 106 f. (Letter by Wordsworth of 28 May 1825).

9. See, for example, J. Hick, *Evil and the God of Love*, London: Macmillan, and New York: Harper and Row, 1966; Austin Farrer, *Love Almighty and Ills Unlimited*, London: A. and C. Black 1962.

10. G. Seaver, *Edward Wilson of the Antarctic*, London: Murray 1933; *Edward Wilson: Nature-Lover*, London: Murray 1937.

11. F. von Hügel, *Selected Letters*, London: Dent, and New York: Dutton 1931, p. 268.

12. M. Quoist, *Prayers of Life*, Dublin: Gill 1961; and *The Christian Response*, Dublin: Gill 1965.

4 Praying and Informal Groups

People who are unsure of God can begin, if they wish, to pray in the broad sense in which we have used that word. But their intellectual integrity will not allow them to evade for ever what Hans Urs von Balthasar has called the 'God-question of modern man'.[1] I cannot tackle this question adequately in a small book on prayer, but it may be useful if I mention two difficulties I have run across in my own experience.

God as Projection

The first time I can remember having difficulty with believing in God was while I was a theological student. My own unbelief resulted from a genuine misunderstanding of psychology. I was quite taken in by the suggestion that men believe in God as Father only because their subconscious desires create and project for them a father-figure in order to give them some kind of security in this bleak, ever-changing world. This figure, I was then convinced, had no objective reality. It was like a mirage of water which thirsty travellers think they see in a desert. It did not at that time occur to me that psychology, just because it has deliberately limited its field of study to the human personality, does not investigate any reality apart from ourselves. Psychology may well explain how we come to desire a father-figure, but psychology itself cannot tell us whether or not there is Being with fatherlike care for us. An analogy may make this clearer. Physiology can explain why we become ravenously hungry, but physiology itself cannot tell whether there is anything in the cupboard for us to eat or not! This is in a necessarily over-simplified way what happened to me, but eventually I emerged out of that spell of unbelief. No doubt Freud and others tell us some very useful things about our human nature; but, as Dr Stafford-Clark, the distinguished English psychologist, has written, 'There is nothing about a belief in psychiatry which makes impossible belief in God.'[2]

God-of-the-Gaps

Later on I nearly slipped into the mistake of regarding God chiefly as the explanation of the otherwise inexplicable, the God-of-the-gaps. Some people argue – and I was once among them – for belief in God from the gaps in our present human knowledge. For example, they now say that, because no one can show how life has emerged in the course of evolution, therefore there must be a God in order to inject life at some moment into inanimate matter. They seem oblivious of the confident expectation that scientists may soon in their laboratories produce from non-living materials simple forms of living creatures. Then the scientists will have closed one more of the gaps in human knowledge. To base one's faith in God on these diminishing gaps in human knowledge is clearly misguided.

This is only the edge of a more serious mistake. Most of the traditional grounds popularly given for believing in God are other instances of this shaky God-of-the-gaps argumentation. For example, it used to be asked, 'Why are there these apparent uniformities, patterns and designs in nature?' and the answer was, 'It can only be because there is God the great designer'. Or again it was asked, 'Why is there a sense of right and wrong in all men?' and it was replied, 'We can find no other reason than that there must be a God, a moral governor, who implanted this conscience in all men.' It is only a small step further to maintain that this God is more concerned with man's servile obedience than with man's fullness of life – a concept of God which has justifiably provoked man's defiance and rejection of this kind of theism. Even without going to such extremes, this sort of argumentation led to a concept of God as One who was in some sense 'beyond' men and 'beyond' the universe, though not necessarily as One who was crudely 'up there' or 'out there'. Yet he was certainly thought of as some kind of 'external' God, a third entity; or, to put it clumsily, we might speak of three distinct entities – God, the universe, ourselves.

I have greatly over-simplified, if not parodied, this way of making deductions about God out of the gaps of our knowledge. These deductions have never been claimed by prudent scholars to be demonstrative proofs of God's existence, but only signposts and indications: and, when carefully stated, they are not without their value.

But fresh ways of proceeding are now being developed, which build not on the gaps of our knowledge, but on a wider and deeper study of human experience and of the whole process of evolution. God is now spoken of as he who in different ways interpenetrates all things, who surrounds, supports and challenges us. He is not of course thought of anthropomorphically, as a celestial emperor. He is in many ways quite beyond our knowing. Personal language is used, because it is the least inadequate language. Personal relationship is the nearest description we can make of our potential relationship with him. But we speak of God as Being, not *a* being, nor a kind of third entity beside the universe and ourselves. This is what Paul said at Athens: 'In God we live and move and have our being' (Acts 17.28). This, in contrast to the watered-down theism of popular teaching, is what the classical teachers of the Christian faith and the great men and women of prayer have also maintained. For example, the great St Augustine wrote, 'Since nothing that is could exist without thee, thou must in some way be in all that is.'[3] This understanding of God needs, of course, to be filled in by what is disclosed in Jesus and by what is genuinely known among believers. This whole development is described by Dr John Macquarrie,

Professor of Systematic Theology at Union Seminary, New York:

Criticisms of traditional theism are being met by the development of new forms of theism, and these in the long run will lead to a better and deeper understanding of Christian faith as a whole. Tillich, Hartshorne, Ogden, Herzog, Dewart – these are just a few names of men who, well aware of the inadequacies of traditional theism, are trying, in various ways and with varying degrees of success, to explicate the idea of God so that men today can know his reality.[4]

Hans Urs von Balthasar may be right when he goes so far as to say:

The frightening phenomenon of modern atheism may, among other things, be a forcible measure of providence to bring back mankind, and especially Christendom, to a more adequate idea of God.[5]

Prayer has gone dead for many people because their concept of God was so inadequate.

For God is either the fullness of fullness, the value of all that is valuable, the wholeness of wholeness, the life of life, or he is nothing.[6]

This new approach reminds us that there are at least two ways of knowing, equally valid in their own sphere. We might call them knowing-with-detachment and knowing-through-involvement. The first is the method of natural science and technology with its meticulous observation as impersonal as possible, with its logical deductions and with the clarity of its scientific conclusions. In the present age we are amazed and perhaps overawed by its fantastic achievements. So men may naturally wish for similar detached observation and clarity of demonstration when we speak of God and of our grounds for belief in him. I must confess I do, perhaps because I began my life as a physicist. But we must declare that this way is impossible.

If we are to come to be sure of God, it is by the other kind of knowing: knowing-through-involvement. It is not only in our relationship with God, but also in aesthetic experience and in human relationships that knowing-through-involvement is the appropriate and only effective way of knowing.

Where is scientific clarity in Picasso or cool detachment in human love? The methods of geometry with their QED (= *quod erat demonstrandum*) are here completely out of place. It is by faith that we can come to know God. We must come clean on that. But faith is not credulity. Faith includes assent to statements about reality, yet faith is far more than that. Faith is much more like being open to a friend, having confidence in him and committing yourself to him. Faith of this kind clearly requires some observable evidence but it goes beyond the bare demands of reason. Faith is supra-rational, but not anti-rational. Faith may sometimes be a leap, but never a blind leap.

I have only been able to touch on these profound questions. They are dealt with in another book in this series, *Who is God?* by D. W. D. Shaw, and also in *The Reality of God* by S. M. Ogden, in *Studies in Christian Existentialism* by John Macquarrie, and in *The Existence of God*, edited by John Hick, which gives some well-chosen extracts from philosophers for and against theism. Most people need some tutor or friend to guide them through the maze of this discussion. Many could be further helped by belonging to a small informal group.

I would like to write about two kinds of groups. I am not happy about my choice of names for them, but I am going to call one kind dialogue groups and the other kind fellowship (or *koinonia*) groups. I would like to say at once and quite firmly what they are not. They are not designed as therapeutic groups. In some circles in the United States I found that you could not use the word 'group' without it being assumed that you are thinking of some group-therapy or sensitivity training. I am not denying that those groups also may have their uses, but they are not the groups I have in mind. Nor are these groups intercession-circles of the traditional kind, though they, too, have their place in the life of the church. Neither of these groups that I am speaking about are meant to be 'debating societies', though I am all for seeing the various sides of any question and engaging in vigorous discussion. The two kinds of groups I have in mind should consist normally of between six and ten people, and it is vital that they should all meet regularly. The two types, the dialogue group and the *koinonia* group, are quite distinct; the latter might sometimes grow out of the former, but it would be disastrous to try to force such a development. I have a hunch that *both* types of group will be very valuable for some years to come, the former to keep believers in touch with the contemporary outlook and the latter to keep alive the inner vitality of believers.

Dialogue group

A dialogue group would normally consist of believers and non-believers and probably some who would not be ready to classify themselves at all. They would need to meet regularly, but perhaps not very frequently, over a considerable period of time. I think that each member should commit himself at least for an initial period of two or three or four months. Unless all are regular at the meetings, not much is likely to emerge. They would need to come to know one another sufficiently well to be able to share freely, frankly and humbly their convictions and experiences. No one would put any pressure on anyone else to change his opinions. Any habitual arguer would be quite out of place. They would never think of one another in the categories of teachers and learners, for everyone would probably gain insight and enrichment from this experience. I would suggest as a wide, over-all theme for their discussions 'What is Man?', 'Man and his needs', or some such title, but I should make it clear from the beginning that I expected that at some point the question of prayer would be raised in some form or other.

I myself have had some small experience of four groups of this kind, and I have certainly learned from them a good deal about prayer. A most useful member in one of these groups was an agnostic psychiatrist who helped us to make useful distinctions about matters we too often confuse. He could not on intellectual grounds pray in any normally accepted way, but he greatly appreciated the positive role which prayer has in many believers' lives. He said that true prayer was not something with which believers cushioned themselves against the stark realities of life, but that it was a quest for the purpose of life, for the individual's place in that purpose, and for authentic relationships with others, in which there was giving as well as receiving. When I decided to include this chapter in this book, I wrote to many friends to ask them if they had experience of similar groups. I drew an almost complete blank, but all encouraged me to go on with this method and said that they thought that I was on to something important. Although I cannot yet marshal much evidence to commend it, I have had enough experience myself to invite others with some confidence to join in exploration of its possibilities. Each group must work out its own methods. But one thing I would suggest is that there should be at some point in each meeting a time of silence for personal reflection; it might be a couple of minutes, or it might be a quarter-of-an-hour. Not all things can be solved by discussion.

Some of these groups may not exist for very long. That is nothing to worry about. We live at a time when people often do not stay long in one place; in their studies and in their work they move quite frequently. Also, many now live full lives and find it difficult to undertake to be at regular meetings. All these groups are experimental. It is better to close a group down if, after a reasonable time, nothing much seems to be happening. There are five things, all or some of which would, I hope, emerge in these groups.

First, by discussing subjects like 'man and his total needs', we might become more aware in our daily lives and responsibilities of that supreme reality, whom believers call God. This book is being written in that conviction. The great focus of the disclosure of that reality is, I believe, in and through Jesus Christ. But I am also profoundly sure, to quote the words of Martin Buber, one of the most discerning of modern Jewish thinkers:

> God speaks to man through the things and beings that he sends into a man's life: man answers by the ways in which he deals with these same things and beings.[7]

The kind of questions we may find ourselves facing might then be these: if we apply the name God to the supreme reality, does he confront us in all things and beings or only in beneficent things, beings and events? Do we need to respond consciously to the supreme reality or do we just do our plain duty without deeper reflection? Is prayer part of this response? If so, what kind of prayer? Believers may need to remind themselves, as Dr Arthur Vogel of the American Nashotah House Seminary has said:

> There is no point in denying that much of what passes for prayer is actually reverie and wish-projection; Christians must learn that such so-called 'prayer' contradicts both their nature and God's.[8]

The second result I should hope for, from such a group, might be the sharpening of the members' faculties to perceive the signs of this great reality. What prevents this perception is not only intellectual but also interpersonal difficulties. We know that these inward defects and blind spots sometimes prevent us from seeing our neighbours' needs, so it may be that they also keep us from being aware of the signs of the divine reality. St Thomas Aquinas has a fine sentence in his work *Contra Gentiles*:

> For a man to be open to divine things he needs tranquillity and peace: now mutual love, more than anything else, removes the obstacles to peace.[9]

It is mutual love (*dilectio mutua*) which creates the tranquillity of mind, which in turn is the condition of truly waiting upon God (*vacare Deo*). This in effect is what the First Letter of John says:

> Everyone who loves is a child of God and knows God, but the unloving know nothing of God   (1 John 4.7 NEB)

The growth of friendship in the group, which of course is a good thing in itself and not a mere means to an end, should help members to be more open not only to one another but also to what Wordsworth meant in the lines:

> The earth and every common sight
> To me did seem
> Apparelled in celestial light.

It might be useful for such groups to have not only discussion but also meals together sometimes. Groups of this quality cannot be 'organized', but many people nowadays seem to be looking for this kind of companionship.

Thirdly, I should hope that these groups would become increasingly conscious that they are part of a far wider movement. The danger is always there that they may subtly become inward-turned coteries. They must always be awake to the invisible companionship of many other seekers. They need to see their links across space and across time. This is why they might fit into their programme a reading together of first-hand writing and published diaries and letters of other seekers and men of prayer. A group in the United States chose the *Serious Call* of William Law, the eighteenth-century English scholar and mystic, for no better reason than that none of them had read it before; they each bought a copy and it became a stimulus to them for months. Some groups have found that it gives form to their exploration if they write and circulate their reflections. All self-conscious effort should be evaded. But such papers might turn out to be of value to wider circles.

Fourthly, one of the aims of the group might be to help members to live their lives – perhaps I had better use a non-religious word – 'in perspective'. For non-believers this would mean arranging the priorities of one's life and responsibilities and living with a sense of proportion. Most of us would profit by this. There are plenty of people who do much less by doing too much. This is not a problem only of our own times. Even in the seventeenth-century

Archbishop Fénelon advised a nobleman at the court of Louis XIV to live a full life leisurely:

> You are always in a hurry to go from one occupation to another, while at the same time each particular thing takes you too far. You should say what has to be said in two words, instead of taking so many means to convince men. Such calm and leisure will forward your affairs in a way that eagerness and forced efforts will never do.[10]

Christians might say that for men to live 'in perspective' means to live in the light and power of God's disclosed purpose and to ask, in the words of an Anglican prayer, for 'a right judgment in all things'.

Fifthly, the group might decide to commit itself to some definite, even if small, service and action. This would be a healthy realism. It sometimes happens that members of a group who cannot express themselves in any sort of God-language take this social commitment very seriously. Is this not prayer in our wider sense of exploration of reality and engagement in life? Perhaps some of these groups might find useful guide-lines from the *politische Nachtgebet* (the political night prayer) which has now been held regularly in Cologne for a year or more. It gathers together Catholics, Protestants and many without any religious ties. It is on a far larger scale than any of the groups discussed in this chapter. It usually meets in a large Catholic or Protestant church. The word 'political' is used widely; this is clear from its themes: Czechoslovakia, Vietnam, immigrant workers, the homeless, financial speculation, sexuality, illness in modern society, and problems of students. The meeting usually begins with readings. These are sometimes, but not always, from the Bible. For instance, at a meeting to consider the penal system a passage was read from Maimonides, a Jew of the twelfth century, including the words, 'When you punish someone, you make him your brother.' Next, concrete evidence about the problem is given; this has been previously prepared by a team assisted by experts in the particular subject. Then all are encouraged to join in the discussion. Finally, definite action is, if possible, decided on; for example, after the discussion on the penal system a working team to help prisoners was set up in Cologne.

One of its founders has described the principles of this prayer in this way. Prayer does not expect the situation to be changed by miracles. Prayer prepares man to take his proper responsibility for the world. For this he needs accurate knowledge, so the first step in this prayer is information. The evidence needs to be weighed, so the second step in this prayer is discussion. Prayer helps us to see solutions which do not yet exist, but which we should bring about; therefore, the third step in this prayer is the consideration of possible action. Further these people express in prayer their desire for the coming kingdom of righteousness and fraternity. So prayer keeps awake their hunger for this kingdom. It helps to keep man human even if his plans are frustrated, and it restrains him from complaining in despair that the world has no meaning.

Fellowship group

The second type of group is the prayer fellowship group. It may possibly develop naturally out of a dialogue group. The purpose of this second type is not only intercession, nor is it only fellowship in a rather self-conscious way. If somehow we could keep the word *koinonia* from sounding rather artificial and precious, perhaps we could keep this New Testament word. It stands for something distinct and is practically untranslatable. It means that quality of companionship which comes from sharing the deep things of life together, including the experience of prayer. The word fellowship sounds shallow, rather matey and self-conscious: community suggests rather too sharply defined boundaries and too much structure. Even if we cannot conveniently use the word *koinonia*, we can keep it in our minds and in our planning. I presume that the members of these latter groups will not be tentative enquirers, but men and women who have come to confidence in God and for whom prayer in some form is a meaningful part of their lives. Even so, there may be great diversity in these groups; and the deepening of their fellowship 'may be impeded by too immediate an insistence on togetherness'.[12] We might see prototypes of these groups in the *koinonia* of the first Christians in Jerusalem (Acts 2.44–47) and in the house-gatherings referred to in the New Testament (Rom. 16.5; 1 Cor. 16.19; Col. 4.15; Philemon 1.2). This is not in any sense archaizing, artificially reproducing the patterns of the first century. It is a desire to infuse the dynamism of first-century Christianity into the church of the latter part of the twentieth century. In the future these small groups may be practically all that there is of a structured church. If, as I think more likely, the church will in many places keep its territorial pattern of parishes, then I am convinced that these parishes will need to be honeycombed with these informal dynamic groups.

David Jenkins, in the postscript to his Bampton Lectures in Oxford, *The Glory of Man*, emphasized the vital importance of these groups in the strategy of the church. He had used his lectures to deal with the question 'What is truly involved in believing in Jesus Christ?' and to help people to work out their own answers. Then he declared:

> People will be persuaded to take up this question only in so far as they come across groups of persons who are attempting to be believers in Jesus Christ and who are displaying a style of life and a manner of involvement in practical realities which are *prima facie* authentic, i.e. have something about them which invite further attention. On matters of fundamental importance, persons must gain a hearing for arguments. Christians, therefore, cannot hope to regain evangelistic effectiveness simply by renovating the terms or the types of their argument. We have to demonstrate authentic practice before we can hope for effective preaching. And this is entirely in the logic of the things concerning Jesus. Jesus was discovered to be the Word of God and the Logos of the cosmos in and through his personal embodied living. God makes himself known in human practice.[13]

I myself am here concerned with what kind of prayer should be at the heart of this *koinonia*. In the next chapter

I will suggest how an individual group might work out its own pattern of prayer. But these two necessities of relevant living witness and authentic prayer are interdependent. 'Prayer is not something you do,' Canon J. V. Taylor has written out of his involvement in Africa and in Britain 'It is a style of living'.[14]

NOTES

1. The original German title of his book *Science, Religion and Christianity* (see ch. 2, note 7).

2. David Stafford-Clark, in: P. Mairet (ed.), *Christian Essays in Psychiatry*, London: SCM Press 1956, p. 28.

3. *Confessions*, I 1 2, ed. F. J. Sheed, London: Sheed and Ward 1944.

4. John Macquarrie, *God and Secularity*, Philadelphia: Westminster Press 1967, and London: Lutterworth Press 1968, p. 109.

5. von Balthasar, *op. cit.*

6. David E. Jenkins, *Living with Questions*, London: SCM Press 1969, p. 24.

7. Martin Buber, quoted in H. Küng (ed.), *Life in the Spirit*, New York: Sheed and Ward 1968, p. 73.

8. A. A. Vogel, *Is the Last Supper Finished? Secular Light on a Sacred Meal*, New York: Sheed and Ward 1968, p. 35.

9. St Thomas Aquinas, *Contra Gentiles*, Book 3, ch. 117.

10. F. Fénelon, *Letters to Men*, ed. N. L. Sidney Lear, London: Longmans 1907, Letter lxviii, pp. 122 f.

11. *Koinonia*, which occurs eighteen times in the New Testament, does not mean merely human fellowship, it means basically sharing together something which comes from God. Believers have fellowship not only with one another, but with the Father and the Son (1 John 1.3). They share together in the Spirit (II Cor. 13.14: Phil. 2.1). They also share together in Christ (I Cor. 1.9), in his sufferings as a prelude to his resurrection (Phil. 3.10), and in the sacrament (I Cor. 1.16). They partake together in faith (Philemon 1.6) and in the gospel (Phil. 1.5). They express this given unity by voluntarily sharing their possessions (Acts 2.42–45; Rom. 15.26; II Cor. 8.4, 9.13; Heb. 13.16). *Koinonia* 'is the sharing of a common life whose source is in God', L. S. Thornton, *Common Life in the Body of Christ*, London: Dacre Press 1944, p. 6.

12. Charles Davis, 'Outdated and Modern Ways of Worship', a paper read at a Faith and Order consultation on 'Worship in a Secular Age', 8–13 September 1969, available in cyclostyled form from WCC, Geneva.

13. David E. Jenkins, *The Glory of Man*, London: SCM Press, and New York: Charles Scribner's Sons 1967, p. 115.

14. John V. Taylor, *CMS News-Letter*, June 1968, p. 4.

5 Praying Together

If the two kinds of informal groups described in the previous chapter wish to spend part of their time together in some sort of prayer, how should they set about it? In this chapter I draw upon the experience of Dietrich Bonhoeffer and also on the experience of the Taizé community.

First, however, I think I should underline what Professor Charles Davis has said recently at a Geneva consultation on 'Worship in a Secular Age' about this kind of prayer:

> There are no rules here. Any form of sharing which contributes to growth together in the realization of personal faith is acceptable: conversation, discussion, silence, reading, singing, group action or common prayer. Because of their personal basis, communities will differ widely, and any feeling of obligation to adopt a particular manner of procedure should be resisted. A fair time may elapse before any direct form of worship is possible together.[1]

My own feeling is that both types of group will probably soon come to appreciate at most meetings a time of silence for personal reflection. Gradually they might wish to extend this silence into verbal prayer, at first perhaps only by stating quietly and briefly what they are grateful for and what they feel deeply concerned about, and then later perhaps by joining together in some more structured prayer. The *koinonia* group would, I expect, be much more likely to make this further development. But it is of the very essence of this exploring into prayer that every type of group should discover its own way and its own pace.

About what form this structure might possibly take Dietrich Bonhoeffer has some interesting things to say. They are all the more interesting because they did not come out of a static ecclesiastical setting. He has proved to be one of the most disturbing thinkers of this century. When only thirty-nine years old, he was executed at Schönberg, almost within sound of the gunfire of the American forces overrunning that part of Germany in April 1945. He had returned from lecturing in the States in one of the last ships to sail before war broke out. Although an anti-Nazi, he was determined to be with his own people and to share their trials. Forbidden to preach, write or speak on the radio, he ran an underground training centre at Finkenwalde near the Baltic for young pastors of the Confessing church, which refused to submit to Hitler's directions. Then the Nazi authorities suppressed the centre and Bonhoeffer was arrested: he had two years in prison. On the day of his execution an English army officer was with him and he said, 'Bonhoeffer was one of the very few men that I have ever met to whom his God was real and ever close to him'.[2] As a theologian, Dietrich Bonhoeffer had thrown out ideas that are still puzzling, rocking and stimulating the Christian church. Through all his experiences there was one thing he hung on to, and that was the importance of the small group of believers and of prayer as a source of its vitality.

Framework

For those who would like a rough framework for their praying together, I would suggest four elements: a few moments of reflection and silence; a psalm or hymn to express the unity of the group; a reading, usually from the Scriptures; and some sharing together of gratitude and of concern for our neighbours and the world. Bonhoeffer made practically the same suggestions about group prayer and its structure in his book *Life Together*, which summarized his experience after the Finkenwalde centre was closed:

Different fellowships will require different forms of worship; this is as it should be. But every common devotion should include the word of Scripture, the hymns of the church, and the prayer of the fellowship.[3]

I would like to elaborate a little on these four elements. About the first, no more need be said except that it means 'unwinding', stepping for a moment out of the rush of life. Some might like to put this into biblical words, such as 'In quietness and confidence shall be your strength' (Isa. 30.15).

The second element would be some words to express and perhaps to deepen the sense of unity of the group and of its solidarity with the great company of believers and seekers which transcends the boundaries of space and time. For this the songs and canticles of the church and especially certain selected psalms would be an obvious choice. Bonhoeffer, typically modern man as he was, could write from his prison cell: 'I read the psalms every day, as I have done for years; I know them and love them more than any other book.'[4] But superficiality is always a danger. Bonhoeffer said, 'The new song is sung first in the heart. Otherwise it cannot be sung at all.'[5] But today's world knows the force of protest songs.

The third element would be some reading, usually but not only from the Bible. Then for a few minutes the insights suggested by the reading might be shared. Enough silence for reflection would be essential. The aim of this reading and reflection is to help us to view life 'in perspective' or, as Christians would say, in the light of God's general disclosure of his purpose. If any group were proposing to meet regularly and frequently, they might plan some systematic and consecutive reading of Scripture. They should at least consider one of Bonhoeffer's recommendations:

> Because the Scripture is a *corpus*, a living whole, the so-called *lectio continua* or consecutive reading must be adopted for Scripture reading in fellowship. Consecutive reading of Biblical books forces everyone who wants to hear to put himself, or to allow himself to be found, where God has acted once and for all for the salvation of men. We become a part of what once took place for our salvation. What we call our life, our troubles, our guilt, is by no means all of reality; there in the Scriptures is our life, our need, our guilt, and our salvation. We must not grudge the time and the work that it takes.[6]

The fourth element would be an opportunity to express both gratitude and concern for our immediate relationships and neighbourhood, and also on wider issues. This might require more discussion, silent reflection, prayer (fairly spontaneous or more structured) and, at least sometimes, a decision on what action should be taken. Bonhoeffer was insistent on the value of concern and mutual prayer:

> A Christian fellowship lives and exists by the intercession of its members for one another, or it collapses. He who denies his neighbour the service of praying for him denies him the service of a Christian.[7]

If the members of some of these groups are living in the same college or hostel, or if they are working in the same hospital, school, factory, office or group of studios, or if their homes are close together, they might consider meeting every day or on most days. They would probably wish to know what suitable material is available for them to use as a basis for their own daily pattern of concern and prayer. One admirable scheme of this kind, designed originally for members of Fitzwilliam College, Cambridge, is called *Daily Prayer* and is available in cyclostyled form.[8]

When members of this kind of group cannot be at their meetings for prayer, they often link themselves in spirit with their group by using personally the same scheme of prayer or at least part of it. As long as this is not allowed to become a burden, it can be a welcome bond, strengthening both the individual and the group. Dietrich Bonhoeffer knew the value of this when he was in his prison cell:

> Before I go to sleep I repeat to myself the verses that I have learnt during the day, and at 6 a.m. I like to read psalms and hymns, think about you all, and know that you are thinking of me.[9]

The office of the Taizé community

Another very fine scheme, though worked out in more detail, comes from the Taizé community.

It was at the end of the war that the Taizé brothers came from Geneva and settled almost unknown in what was then the rather derelict village of Taizé on a hill looking across a spacious Burgundy countryside. Now everyone knows them as a Protestant, quasi-monastic community. Then they were about half a dozen, now they are about eighty from most of the Evangelical churches in western Europe. At first sight the brothers appear rather traditional. But they are deeply involved in the world. They have set up a farming co-operative at Taizé and have transformed the economic life of their area. About half their number are away from Taizé; they live together and earn their living in small fraternities. Some of them live with two or three Catholic Franciscans in a black, proletarian district in Chicago in the centre of racial tensions. Another small fraternity is at Recife in one of the poorest parts of Brazil. Others have lived through all the troubles in Algeria. They live amongst their neighbours undistinguished by dress or housing. They wish to form cells of Christian love and concern in some of the more difficult spots of the modern world.

One of the strongest links they have with one another and with their base at Taizé is a shared pattern of praying together; this they call the Office de Taizé.[10] It was produced by the method of trial and error. They worked it out section by section on cyclostyled copies. It is, as it claims to be, the fruit of a living experience of prayer. It is clearly designed primarily for men who are convinced and are committed to God and his kingdom. But these are not men isolated and sheltered from the world, they are in the thick of the world, deeply concerned with the problems and opportunities of today: 'the third world', the student world, the problems of industry and of co-operative farming. Young people visit the Taizé centre each summer and camp there in their thousands. So this pattern of prayer must be usable not only in their modern, functional church at Taizé and in the charming mediaeval village church, which the Roman Catholic authorities allow this community to use, but also in their small fraternities in very secular settings. Although this scheme of prayer is in the first place the corporate prayer of the Taizé community, it is used with modifications all over the world by friends and sympathizers of the Taizé brothers. Even some Roman Catholic communities are officially allowed by their church authorities to use it. This office has its roots in the deep traditions of the churches; some people might think it carries over a little too much tradition. It spans many of the differences between the churches, for the ecumenical spirit of Taizé is summed up in its principle, *Aie la passion de l'unité*, 'Have passion for unity'. But these patterns of prayer, though they are rooted in tradition, express the needs of the contemporary world. Further, because it is not the official form of a church, it is flexible, provisional (a favourite word of the Taizé brothers) and always open to revision. It explicitly claims for itself only to be one step forward in the rediscovery of the worship of the church and in the search for the unity of all Christians.

The Office of Taizé provides a form, which can be used in whole or in part, for every morning and evening of the year. (Many friends of Taizé use a short part of the office, a psalm or a reading, once or twice a day, as their valued link with the community.) Each form follows the four steps in praying together outlined earlier in this chapter. First, the words of the opening call to reflection and prayer are excellently chosen. They set our lives and our praises in the perspective of God's care for mankind. What Christians regard as the most significant signs of God's care for his people, that is, the coming of Christ, his life-work, his dying, his glorification and the coming of his Spirit, are made one after another the themes of these introductory words during the course of the year. The variety and the richness of these introductions is one of the most attractive features of this collection. Secondly, the singing or the saying of one or two psalms gives to those who are present a sense of unity and also a link with those who today or in the past have desired to be God's people in prayer and in action. Thirdly, there are short readings from the Bible. These set out what God has done, is doing and will do for the world and the church. Their aim is again to give perspective to our lives today. Each morning there are two readings, one from the Old Testament and one from the Gospels, and then each evening one reading either from the Acts of the Apostles or the Epistles of the New Testament. In this way most of the Old Testament is read once in three years, and the Gospels and the rest of the New Testament are each read every year. After the readings there is a time for reflection and also some well-chosen verses which echo and re-echo a theme intended to help people meditate on the passage. Fourthly, there are thanksgivings and intercessions, in the form of verses and responses, related to the world and the church of today.

These forms are wonderfully adaptable. I have used them around a meal-table on a winter's evening with a few Taizé brothers working for a time in an English industrial town. Equally I have used them out of doors on a June evening with young people at a conference overlooking the Lake of Geneva. They are used day by day, morning and evening, at the Taizé centre, in winter, in the centuries-old village church and, in the summer, in the brothers' new church, significantly called the Church of the Reconciliation. This new church was designed by a Taizé brother, who is an architect, and was built largely by German students as a sign of the post-war reconciliation. Here, on a summer's evening, there are often three or four hundred people, many of them students, grouped around some forty of the brothers of Taizé. The singing of the psalms goes with an *élan*. The hymns are often sung simultaneously in French, German and English from the hymn-book *Cantate Domino*. Daily in the summer this is an international and interchurch assembly in praise and prayer. By no means all who are there are believers, and this worship seems often to be the place of birth or rebirth of faith. The prior of the Taizé community has said, 'Haven't we been discovered and recognized by so many agnostics through our liturgical prayer?'[11] I have noticed this myself. On one of my visits there I met a typically vigorous young German of about twenty. He had been there for some weeks on a work camp, helping to build some simple accommodation for the hundreds of people who wish to spend a few days at Taizé in retreat and reflection. He told me that his father was about to arrive and drive him back to Hamburg. He said he did not know what he would have to say because for six years he had declared himself to be an atheist, but at Taizé he had found in the worship an inspiration and a strength. He said to me – and I could hardly believe my ears – 'Since soon after arriving here, I have day by day been waiting for the next service to come round'.

An ecumenical daily office

Many churches have designed similar patterns of prayer. When in the sixteenth century the Anglican Book of Common Prayer was compiled, its main author, Archbishop Cranmer, hoped that it would form just this kind of daily prayer for lay people. That is why he directed that the parish priest should morning and evening have the church bell rung so that 'the people may come to hear God's Word and to pray with him'.[12] But as weekday prayer for the laity it has hardly come off. Roman Catholic priests are trying to adapt for the use of the laity many parts of their daily service book, the Breviary, which is in the course of being revised in very significant ways. For example, an experimental revision has been officially authorized in France, which provides not only biblical readings and passages from the great scholars of the early church, but also passages from present-day theologians such as Yves Congar and Karl Rahner, and even from non-Catholics like Roger Schutz, the prior and inspirer of Taizé, and Martin Luther King of the Civil Rights movement.

Another significant development in Britain is the recent publication of an ecumenical Daily Office of prayer for morning and evening. It was drawn up by official representatives of the Church of England, the Church of Scotland, the Baptist Union of Great Britain and Ireland, the Congregational Church in England and Wales, the Episcopal Church in Scotland, the Methodist Church, the Presbyterian Church of England and the Churches of Christ, with an observer from the Roman Catholic church. It has resemblances to the Taizé office. It has, of course, no official authority unless any of these churches authorize it. Some Anglicans would like to see it recognized as an alternative to their Prayer Book daily offices. Each of these new offices finishes with an informal scheme of thanksgivings and prayers, deliberately left 'open-ended'. I can see this book being useful to groups or to individuals in one of three ways. Some may wish to use only the daily scheme for informal thanksgivings and intercessions, which forms Appendix A to this book. Some may prefer one office a day, which is outlined in the closing pages of the office book. Others may desire the full office, morning and evening. But all should feel that they are sharing in the same ecumenical fellowship of prayer.

The rationale of the daily office

Many groups, *koinonia* groups as well as dialogue groups, will not be drawn to structured prayer, still less to an office of prayer. Yet there are features of praying together which everyone might well consider, and then accept, or modify, or reject. The rationale of all schemes of prayer of this type is well set out in this ecumenical *Daily Office* book in the introductory essay by Stephen Winward, a Baptist minister. It is a sign of our ecumenical times when a Baptist provides the *raison d'être* for what used to be considered a predominantly Catholic pattern of prayer. I will try to put into my own words what he says. Four reasons are given for these patterns of prayer. They can lift us out of an excessive and depressing individualism; they can give us the joy of celebration; they can deepen our sense of responsibility; and they can show us how to make the most of our time. Everyone must, of course, weigh these reasons up for himself and draw his own conclusions.

First, these patterns can lift us out of an individual narrowness of prayer and often out of an individual groping in doubt. They remind us that we are surrounded with thousands of other people in various stages of belief and half-belief who, like us, wish to concern themselves with the true good of their neighbours and with the purpose of God as far as they can discern it. By sharing in these patterns of prayer we are drawn into the great company of those who are searching, desiring, praying and going into action.

Since we are surrounded by so great a cloud of witnesses, let us run with perseverance the race that is set before us (Heb. 12.1)

This can renew our vision. This can reinvigorate us, particularly when our faith and energy are low.

Secondly, these patterns of prayer can bring us the joy of celebration. Men are so constituted that they not only need to care for and serve their neighbours, but also to celebrate with joy their achievements together.

The glorious Majesty of the Lord our God be upon us: Prosper thou the work of our hands upon us. O prosper thou our handywork (Psalm 90.17)
O sing unto the Lord a new song, for he has done marvellous things (Psalm 98.1)

Verses like these echo and re-echo as we regularly share in these patterns of prayer and praise. They also remind us – when achievement is delayed or when we might become embittered – that in our service we are working not in a dead materialistic universe, but with the purpose of God, the great reality of the universe. In fact, Harvey Cox, the *avant-garde* theologian, says:

Ultimately radicals would be more effective if now and again they allowed themselves to live, if only on occasion, as though all the things they were struggling for were already accomplished. Theologians might call this a kind of 'proleptic liberation'.[13]

69

Thirdly, the regular use of these patterns of prayer can make us realize that to seek, to desire, to work for the good of others is not a passing inclination, but a definite responsibility which we deliberately accept as men and women. To make this point I would like to digress a moment and look at the words 'office' or 'daily office'. They have been used as a name for these regular patterns of prayer. Many modern Christians do not care much for these words, nor as a matter of fact do I. The word is derived from the Latin *officium*, which means a required duty. It sounds like legalism. On the other hand, we can properly and usefully use the word 'office' as a name for these patterns of prayer if we keep in mind two contemporary uses of the word. To hold office means to have a position which demands or should demand a conscientious discharge of responsibility. An office also describes a place where serious business is or should be transacted. So whenever we join in these daily offices of prayer, we should be reminding ourselves of our responsibilities towards our fellow-men and committing ourselves to action. In our direct responsibility to society we need imagination and passion, but we also need reason, intelligence, determination and staying-power. It is exactly the same in our planned, faithful, genuine prayer, which involves us in action. Love should drive us to concern, to prayer, to responsibility, to action. This love has its spontaneity; it also has, like all love, to find its own *disciplined* strength.

Fourthly, these patterns and offices of prayer help us to make the most of our time. Man needs leisure, relaxation and enjoyment. Yet he also needs a sense of responsibility in the use of time. Time and energy which are consumed in preparing for worship, selecting psalms and biblical passages, might often be better spent in prayer itself or in consequent action. This preparatory work has already been done for us with considerable skill by those who have compiled the offices. Of course some emergency may lead us to substitute some other material or even to omit the office; and at least part of our reflecting and praying should always be spontaneous. But something good has been given to us to use.

A more important point. The times when we join in the office are not times of flight from the world and our responsibilities. They are, or should be, short times, in which we try quietly and deliberately to commit our time to service. *Pars pro toto*. Part as representative of and pledge for the whole. Experience shows that if possible these times should be regular and fairly frequent; short perhaps, but frequent, for they are intended to set and to keep our whole lives in true perspective and genuine commitment. They may not always be at the traditional times of prayer on getting up and going to bed; they may be in a commuters' train, in an office before actual work begins, on a seat in a park or in the quiet of church. But they will not be casual times or sporadic efforts. They will be the heart-beats of our service of men and of the Lord who, we believe, dwells in them and wills to make them and us more truly human.

The Eucharist

Another interesting development in our days is that the eucharist is becoming the focal point for all sorts of Christians and even for those who are on the fringe. It can still speak to and help those who are full of perplexities and doubts. One piece of evidence is hidden away in a paper read by a theological student to priests who had formerly been members of his college. He explained what the eucharist in the college chapel had meant to him even in his most perplexed moments:

The world picture which I then had was one into which the notion of a transcendent God just did not fit. This approach made nonsense of prayer and worship, traditionally understood. Any idea of praying to someone, of talking to someone, of trying to bring one's will into line with God's will was nonsensical. But the *one* service which did make sense was the eucharist, in terms of the gathering of the whole local accepting community round the re-presentation

71

of the self-giving Christ. Gathered together in this context the church is empowered to love and to accept.[14]

The eucharist is, I grant, still interpreted in very varied ways amongst Catholics, Orthodox, Anglicans and Protestants, amongst radicals and traditionalists, though their differences are often less sharp than they used to be. But as earlier in this book I offered a wide preliminary description of prayer as 'exploration of reality and reflective engagement in life', so I would now suggest an equally wide provisional understanding of the eucharist. Here it is: The eucharist is our gathering together to celebrate with gratitude and joy our commitment to Christ and to his coming kingdom. We desire that as a consequence of this celebration we shall be made more and more a caring and a serving community committed to action in the world. This is deliberately wide so that we can all join in this exploration of the eucharist together. Doubtless we shall wish to qualify it and amplify it in our own various ways. There are two points in this statement which I should like to underline.

First, for those who are believers, worship, specially at the eucharist, should be like a joyful party of friends. I know it often is not. But it should be an outburst of gratitude and love. It is a good thing in itself, and not only the means to some practical end. Secondly, the eucharist is essentially a corporate action. This is what many people are rediscovering. The eucharist is something a group does together. We discover its joy (which is not incompatible with sacrifice) by doing it together.

There will presumably always be the need for large-scale eucharists; sometimes the Christians of a diocese or wider area will wish to gather together for the eucharist; there will be in the future ecumenical eucharists at international gatherings of Christians; there will be the large Sunday eucharists of strong centres of Christian life. These eucharists will probably call for a certain grandeur and richness of colour, which is not to be confused with fussy or merely antiquarian ceremonies. It is quite a mistake to think that all modern people always prefer the eucharist plain, bare and utilitarian. This is put in an amusing way by Father Andrew Greeley, a Roman Catholic sociologist at Chicago:

> I note in passing the supreme irony that precisely at the time when the Roman church is under pressure to give up vestments and avoid ceremonies, the world of psychedelia is creating new vestments for its ceremonies, and that precisely at the time that the Roman collar is becoming unfashionable, the turtle-necked sweater and the Nehru jackets have become fashionable. Finally, at precisely the time when bishops are under heavy pressure to yield up their beloved pectoral crosses, new jewelry for men has become the rage. It's an awfully strange world.[15]

Yet these great eucharists will not be able to give to all who are there a strong sense of 'belonging' to one another. Some will inevitably feel like mere specks in a crowd; they will come and go as anonymous individuals. But this is not entirely to be regretted. At a certain stage many seekers rightly wish to be anonymous seekers. Later on these enquirers may be glad of the small informal group.

Among these large-scale eucharists, we must not rule out the possibility of a new style of eucharist derived from the multi-media services, which are now proliferating amongst students in the United States. I attended one of these eucharists at an Episcopalian university chaplaincy centre. We certainly had a sense of community as we sat on the floor packed together like sardines. Rapidly-flashed images on many screens and also a dance group made us vividly aware of the chaotic world in which we live and try to serve. The electronic music was so fortissimo and to me cacophonic that I just gave up trying to make sense of it. Paradoxically I then experienced, not through silence but through an overload of noise, that kind of receptivity which the Roman Catholic philosopher Josef Pieper says is at the heart of worship and contemplation, when we 'look at reality purely receptively – in such a way that things are the measure and the soul is exclusively receptive'.[16] The priest wore brilliant eucharistic vestments. There were clouds of incense. The eucharistic prayer was said, if I caught the words correctly, from the liturgy of St Mark's-in-the-Bouwery.[17] Then we passed to one another long, French-looking rolls of bread and great goblets of wine. It was a feast, like a feast before setting out on a journey. It was a bizarre experience. But these services are being taken seriously enough for a high-level conference of theologians, philosophers, sociologists and literary critics to be held to evaluate their methods. The papers of this consultation have been published under the title *Multi-Media Worship*.[18] Harvey Cox was right when he said:

> This represents the contemporary technological equivalent of the pageants, feasts and bonfires men have staged since the dawn of consciousness. Christianity has nothing against noise and revelry as such. It does suggest, however, that celebration should open man not just to the joy of the senses and the *élan* of the feast itself, but to the larger cosmos of which he is part and to the history he is involved in making.[19]

For many years we have known the value of house-communions in parishes.[20] But now they are happening in an ecumenical way amongst students and other professional and informal groups. For example, another Anglican and I were invited to receive holy communion at a mass in the small house of studies of a Roman Catholic religious community in Berkeley, California. It was early evening, lectures and classes were over, there was a relaxed feeling of celebration and joy. We sat in their common-room around a small table where the celebrating priest sat in his lay clothes. It was clearly the focus of their everyday life together. After the scripture reading, discussion turned naturally on how the demoralizing Vietnam war, so contrary to the gospel, could be brought to an end. We tried to find out what students could actively do. It is not much good apparently in America lobbying individual congressmen and senators on really major issues; and you cannot throw out a government and have a general election as in Britain. Nor is it effective just to go out on to the campus and protest. It is a matter of long planning and co-ordination, and a question of whom you can collaborate with, and what methods you think legitimate. It was a real attempt to see our present responsibilities in true perspective, and really earthed. The intercessions followed naturally and were entirely spontaneous. There was some singing to the quiet strumming of a guitar. We used an admirable canon of the mass from Dutch catholics. The eucharistic bread was scones on a large plate. We stood and passed to one another the chalice, while we were singing a communion song. The sense of joy and *koinonia* was very strong, as well as a determination to take action in the world.

In the next few years there may be very many small groups wishing to celebrate the eucharist together in this kind of way – in offices, in studios, in hostels, and in private houses; and many of them will be ecumenical. In these small groups intercommunion will probably be taken for granted. As their numbers increase, the question whether a layman could preside at these eucharists is bound to be asked. We need first to be clear that it is always the church, the group itself, which corporately celebrates the eucharist. Then it must be remembered that the group at a eucharist is never merely a private group of friends, but is part of the worldwide people of God. If a minister of the church presides it is a reminder that this eucharist is not the action of a coterie, but of the universal church. Yet it is already time that we discussed the possibility of a suitable layman presiding, if a minister were not available for the eucharist. Leslie Houlden, a priest in the catholic tradition of the Anglican church, wrote in a paper prepared for the 1968 Lambeth conference:

There is room for difference of opinion how far these tasks, undeniably associated with the clergy, should be confined to them. Some tasks, such as the pastoral, are not necessarily theirs alone, and it is worth asking whether there is any substantial theological reason why others (such as presiding at the eucharist) should not similarly be regarded as only conventionally their sole province. [21]

This is only one of many new questions which will be raised about the eucharist in the near future. We must be ready to see many styles of eucharist. Some will help certain temperaments, some will help others. But all the eucharists must be not only rejoicing in the Lord but related to the actual world in which we live. Michael Novak has written, 'a man, who offers bread to God when other men starve for lack of bread, has not understood the gospel of Jesus Christ'.[22]

NOTES

1. See chapter 4, note 12.

2. Payne Best, *The Venlo Incident*, p. 180, quoted in Mary Bosanquet, *The Life and Death of Dietrich Bonhoeffer*, London: Hodder and Stoughton, and New York: Harper and Row 1969, p. 272. This book is an excellent introduction to Bonhoeffer.

3. Dietrich Bonhoeffer, *Life Together*, London: SCM Press, and New York: Harper 1954, p. 34.

4. Dietrich Bonhoeffer, *Letters and Papers from Prison*, p. 46.

5. Dietrich Bonhoeffer, *Life Together*, p. 48.

6. *Op. cit.*, p. 43.

7. *Op. cit.*, pp. 45 f.

8. *Daily Prayer* can be had in cyclostyled form from the Revd Peter Nott, Beaconsfield Rectory, Beaconsfield, Bucks.

9. Dietrich Bonhoeffer, *Letters and Papers from Prison*, p. 43.

10. *Office of Taizé* (English Translation), London: Faith Press 1966.

11. Roger Schutz, quoted in G. Moorhouse, *Against All Reason*, London: Weidenfeld and Nicolson 1969, p. 15.

12. 'Concerning the Service of the Church', a prefatory section to the *Book of Common Prayer* according to the use of the Church of England. (These words do not occur in some versions of the Prayer Book used elsewhere in the Anglican Communion.)

13. Harvey Cox, *The Feast of Fools*, Cambridge, Mass.: Harvard University Press 1969, and London: Oxford University Press 1970, p. viii.

14. *Fresh Springs* No. 3, 1965; an occasional paper of Lincoln Theological College, England.

15. A. M. Greeley, *Religion in the Year 2000*, New York: Sheed and Ward 1969, pp. 129 f.; see also a perceptive article by the same author, 'The Sacred and the Psychedelic', *The Critic* (Chicago), April/May 1969.

16. Josef Pieper, *Leisure the Basis of Culture*, London: Faber 1952, p. 104.

17. This liturgy, which is in contemporary language and gives the congregation a large part to play in the eucharist, is given in Appendix B at the end of this book.

18. See note 2 to the Introduction.

19. Harvey Cox, *Feast of Fools*, p. 110.

20. For a practical description and a theological assessment of house communions, see E. W. Southcott, *The Parish Comes Alive*, London: Mowbray 1956; J. A. T. Robinson, *On Being the Church in the World*, Harmondsworth: Penguin Books 1969; A. Shands, *The Liturgical Movement and the Local Church*, London: SCM Press 1965.

21. L. Houlden, 'The Priesthood', in: *Lambeth Essays on the Ministry*, edited by the Archbishop of Canterbury, London: SPCK 1969, p. 45.

22. M. Novak, postscript to Malcolm Boyd (ed.), *The Underground Church*, Baltimore: Penguin Books 1969, p. 276.

6 Bible and Praying

'I am looking for some kind of contemporary prayer, but why should I expect much help from something so remote from modern life as the Bible?' This is typical of much that I have heard in conversations recently with men and women who, though they are unsure about God, are looking for some sort of prayer. But it is not from the Bible that they look for light, but rather from the immediacy of their own experience and from comparing their impressions with their contemporaries. Some have frankly told me that what might 'turn them on to prayer' (as they put it) would not be the Bible but rather a *guru*, a holy man, or multi-media worship, or a meaningful personal relationship, or perhaps some sexual experience or psychedelic drugs.[1]

Objections

Many of these people would admit that there are helpful and moving passages in the Scriptures, like the beatitudes in the sermon on the mount. Practically all of them would agree that there is much to admire in the human life of Jesus. But in general they do not think that the Bible is of much use today. For example, they point first of all to the ferocities in some of the Old Testament stories and commands, like, 'Your eye shall not pity; it shall be life for life, eye for eye, tooth for tooth' (Deut. 19.21). Even the New Testament, they say, is not free from traces of vindictiveness, for example against the persecuting Roman empire. Secondly, they say that much that was thought to be historical is now shown to be mythical or legendary, and that not in the Old Testament only, but probably even in the gospels. Everybody knows this now, they tell us, through TV programmes, theological paperbacks and radically written, religious articles in mass-circulation, secular magazines. Thirdly, they remind us that in the past the Bible has been quoted to support the persecution of witches and the keeping of slaves and also to keep women from having equal rights in society; and they say that even today the Bible is used to oppose reforms which are being pressed for by forward-looking people both within and outside the churches.

I see the point of these objections, though I do not think that they are quite as sweeping as they may appear to be at first sight. But before examining them, I ought to say what I think the main purpose of the Bible is, at least for those who are searching for some way of prayer. And even before doing that I must affirm that it is essential that the scriptures be as rigorously examined and tested as any other historical documents. The German scholar, Günther Bornkamm, is right when he says:

> Without the process of criticism and counter-criticism there is no knowledge of historical truth in the biblical field or in any other.[2]

Purpose

The New Testament documents, after they have been tested in this way, give us reliable and vivid insight into the experience of the first Christian communities. To have their living experience *reactivated* in us is one of the main purposes of our reflecting on the New Testament. It is for us now to share in what they had. They found themselves grasped and possessed by a reality, which took them rather by surprise, as a deep human love sometimes does. This they called 'life in the Spirit'. They were still very much living in the world, but life took on a new dimension. They still had their faults (the book of the Acts of the Apostles and the First Letter to the Corinthians make that clear), but they knew that they were (if the expression may be

79

used) 'turned on to something new'. This was not primarily excitement or ecstasy, but they had a new capacity for love and courage. That is how they managed to begin to 'turn the world upside down' (Acts 17.6) – and this still needs to be done. Tom Baker in another book in this series has justifiably said:

> It cannot be too strongly emphasized that, though the experience of the new life in the Spirit was 'subjective' in the sense that it was directly 'felt', it was in its essence an experience of something 'given', originating in a divine act, not of human contriving.[3]

The first Christians were convinced of this, and they were the primary, if not infallible, observers. This experience emerged from their living, creative memory of Jesus. Anyone, who has shared in a deep personal relationship, knows that there is a world of difference between a living memory of this kind and mere reminiscence about someone. But there was more than memory. The first Christians were utterly convinced that Jesus was risen, was amongst them, was dynamically with them. They were also sure that, through the life, dying and rising of Jesus, God was active at a new level to liberate from fear and egoism both themselves and potentially all mankind. This was the heart of reality. They could not keep it to themselves. It gave them perspective for their lives, commitment to the Lord and his cause, and strength to follow it through.

This does not mean that we should archaize, should idealize a primitive church, and try to live in a rosy-coloured past in a pre-Copernican, pre-Marxist, pre-Freudian golden age. It is quite the contrary. It is that together, in the latter part of the twentieth century, we should participate in the dynamism of the New Testament Christians through our reflecting, praying and living. Dr John Knox has expressed this well:

> The New Testament gives us access to the Christ event only because it makes us, in a real sense, *participants* in the experience of those to whom it was first occurring. As we read the New Testament, we

become witnesses of the original event, *not* by getting 'back to' or beyond the primitive community but by getting *more deeply* into its life. For there is no access to the Christ event except as it is remembered and embodied in that first community.[4]

I must not give the impression that this understanding of the purpose of the New Testament is merely an explanation thought up to meet modern difficulties. It is essentially what the author of St John's Gospel, for example, says about his own aim in writing:

Now Jesus did many other signs in the presence of the disciples, which are not written in this book; but these are written that you may believe that Jesus is the Christ, the Son of God, and that believing you may have life in his name (John 20.30 f.).

For in this passage believing means committing ourselves to Christ as a man through whom God the ultimate reality has broken into everyday life in a peculiarly significant way. This believing is not something completed in a moment. Two German theologians have put this far more penetratingly than I could. Dorothee Sölle says, 'My act of faith is my-allowing-myself-to-be-determined by my encounter with Christ',[5] and to this Rudolf Bultmann adds, 'The decision of faith is never final, it needs constant renewal in every fresh situation.'[6] Further, in this passage, the life, which comes through believing, is not merely human life or only some life beyond death; it stands for the fullness of life lived with one another, with the reality of God and with his disclosure in Christ.[7]

Response

If this is what really matters for us in the scriptures, how do those objections to the Bible now look?

First there is no denying the ferocities and crudities, but they do not worry us; they are, I think, quite peripheral. The Bible is not a monolithically authoritarian volume, it is a library of very varied types of books, written over a span of more than a thousand years. So we should not be surprised at what is primitive in it. Some of these writers will naturally be less perceptive than others. We should expect some general progress in spiritual insight over those centuries.

This follows from the fact that the disclosures of the ultimate reality do not, as it were, come fluttering down from heaven on neatly-typed sheets of paper. That is not how we come to know of the reality of God and of the varied ways in which man can be in contact with that reality. Disclosures come, apparently, not in abstract terms, but intertwined with and focused on concrete events. They come sometimes in political events like the escape of the Hebrews from slavery in Egypt or their later return from exile in Babylonia: sometimes in the experience of a small significant group, like the disciples at the mysterious but focal Easter event or at the Pentecost event at Jerusalem: and sometimes in personal and apparently trivial events, as when the young prophet Jeremiah watched an almond tree breaking into blossom (Jer. 1.11 f.). But there is no disclosure, unless the event coincides with the presence of men who in the words of Martin Noth, the German Old Testament scholar, can 'discern in the events of their own age the beginnings of the operation of a divine plan'[8] – or, as believers would say, men to whom God gives the capacity to discern and to interpret. Even so, what the men discern in these events about God, about his love, power and purpose, they have to express in their own language and imagery, which is inevitably less or more inadequate. Nor is the man only a passive recipient, but as Father Thornton, the rather subtle biblical scholar of the English Community of the Resurrection, said, 'Revelation is always given not only to, but also in and through response'.[9] Perhaps we can begin to understand this, because in a very minor way many of us, who try to write, find that what we have to write sometimes comes to us in the act of writing.

None of these interpreters and writers had perfect spiritual sight. Some in fact seem to have been half blind, and their successors have had to correct their predecessors' half-errors. For instance, the man who originally wrote 'Eye for eye, tooth for tooth' was ahead of his times: he was pleading for equal retaliation instead of unlimited revenge. But of course he was seeing less than half of the whole demand of love; and he was later corrected by Jesus the prophet of Nazareth in his hyperbolic saying:

> You have heard that it was said, 'An eye for an eye and a tooth for a tooth'. But I say to you, Do not resist one who is evil. But if anyone strikes you on the right cheek, turn to him the other also (Matthew 5.38 f.)

So disclosures are real, but seldom are they recorded without distortion. There is nearly always 'a personal equation' to be allowed for. We must always remember this when we read the Bible.

The second objection to the Bible was that much which believers thought to be historical is now shown to be mythical or legendary. There is certainly something in this objection, but each incident must be examined on its own merits. Some parts of the Old Testament which may look like history, such as the story of Jonah, were probably never intended to be more than parabolic stories. Even the biblical authors, who attempted to write history, could not conceivably have had the methods and training of modern historians. This is true of the writers of history of all nations at that time. For the authors of the Old Testament books, the only evidence available was often hundreds of years after the events. They did not even think of themselves as dispassionate historians but as preachers and prophetic leaders; it is significant that in the Hebrew text of the Old Testament the so-called historical books of Samuel and Kings are classified as the books of 'the earlier prophets'. Many Christians readily accept this approach to the Old Testament.

They seem less at ease when these same methods are applied to the New Testament. But a careful study of the four gospels makes it clear that they were not intended as straightforward biographies. If they had been, the authors

83

would presumably have said something about Jesus' personal appearance, and would have unearthed and recorded some incidents in the almost complete gap between the stories of his infancy and the beginning of his life-work. A thorough examination of the gospels makes them look as if they have been put together as collections of sayings and stories, some of them sermon-illustrations, but not arranged in the chronological order in which they happened. They are like a necklace of beads, the string has broken, and the writers have rethreaded the beads in an order which seemed appropriate to them. Nor can we exclude the possibility that prayerful reflections on the words of Jesus by the early Christians are now interwoven with their recollections of his life, specially in St John's Gospel. This is what we might expect, if the early Christians had this strong sense of the Risen Lord still present with them. The American scholar, Dr W. D. Davies, has in fact said:

> We may be more in touch with Jesus himself than if we simply had his words. The dormant meaning of the words has been awakened for us by the Spirit informing the great author of the Fourth Gospel.[10]

We shall have to return to this matter; but historical study today indicates that we have a substantially reliable portrait of Jesus in the gospels. Professor Bornkamm, who comes from the very critical school of German New Testament experts, has written:

> Although the gospels do not speak of the history of Jesus in the way of reproducing the course of his career in all its happenings and stages, in its inner and outer development, nevertheless they do speak of history of occurrence and event. . . . The gospels give abundant evidence of such history. . . . In every layer and in each individual part, the tradition is witness to the reality of its history and the reality of his resurrection.[11]

About the third objection we must frankly admit that, although Christians have done something in the past for moral and social progress, it is undeniable that they have held up and to some extent still hold up further progress by quoting verses of the Bible and often trying to apply them too literally. Again each question – and they are sometimes very complex – must be considered on its own merits.

Our own responsibility is to make a more perceptive use of scripture. The Bible is not meant to provide us with precise solutions to our contemporary problems. We need to find some way of reflecting on scripture so that we participate in the *élan* and vitality of the first Christian communities. That is its function for us. We must guard against taking what Dr Krister Stendahl, the Dean of Harvard Divinity School, calls 'a too close-sighted view' of scripture. We must not forget, he says, that owing to modern scientific and psychological studies 'the distance between the first and the twentieth centuries has drastically widened' and that 'all theology of the twentieth century has to come to terms with this distance'.[12] The New Testament gives us vitality, perspective and some principles. We are then left to work out policies for our own situation. What the first Christians could not do, we often can do. They were an insignificant minority. Nowadays Christians are numerous enough in some countries to have a considerable influence, if they are sufficiently determined, in the struggle for social and political changes. They must, of course, work with other men of goodwill.

The apostle Paul could not in his day make any appreciable change in the social conditions of the Roman empire. Yet through his commitment to Christ he discovered dynamite which we are now in a position to use. The dynamite is in the words of one of his letters, 'There is no such thing as Jew and Greek, slave and freeman, male and female; for you are all *one person* in Christ Jesus' (Gal. 3.28). Potentially this is so for humanity. All that Paul could do in his time was to fight and largely win the battle for equality between Jew and Greek in the first century Christian communities. But he could make no visible impact on the problem of slavery or of the place of women in society. We now have before us all these problems – race, class

85

and sex – on a vaster scale and in untold ramifications. And, if we are determined, we have the vitality and the power to tackle them.

Christ-among-his-own

The findings of modern historical study of the Bible and particularly of the New Testament are then a gain rather than a loss. We have not photographic pictures of the biblical characters, not even of our Lord in Galilee, but perhaps we have something better. Tom Baker puts it well:

> The New Testament provides us with a picture not of Jesus-in-himself but of Christ-in-the-midst-of-his-own, in relation to a great variety of individual and corporate needs, problems and opportunities – spiritual, personal and intellectual. Such a view helps Christians today in their present task of relating the unchanging gospel to a very rapidly changing world.[13]

But we must not try to evade the crucial questions about Christ himself. First, is it not arrogant to claim that Jesus is 'a unique disclosure of ultimate reality?'[14] Is there adequate historical evidence to support this claim? What is the essential content of his disclosure?

There are two kinds of uniqueness, exclusive uniqueness and inclusive uniqueness. The first means: 'I am right and all others are wrong'. Jesus never made such a claim, nor should we ever think of making it for him. His claim – or should we better say his vocation? – was inclusively unique. The faith of his Jewish forefathers was not arrogantly set aside by him; that would have been to claim an exclusive uniqueness. Rather, Jesus gathered up into himself the deepest insights of that Jewish faith, and so his followers saw him to be the completion and focus of that faith; he has a uniqueness which is inclusive. Similarly, to welcome light from other nations is not inconsistent with faith in Christ. In fact St John's Gospel speaks of him as the *Logos* of God, the utterance of God, and also as the light which lightens *every* man. Christ does not disparagingly exclude other lights, but rather includes them. He is not against but with others. In the same way Justin Martyr, the second-century Christian writer, could claim that Plato and the Stoic philosophers shared in the *Logos* that was in Jesus.[15] Dr Norman Pittenger has summarized this truth, 'The incarnation of God in Jesus Christ is *focally* but not exclusively true of him'.[16] So in our day the utterance of God may come to us through men of other faiths and through non-believers. We may learn more from atheists who are seeking reality than from the evasive answers of some Christians. It was of a pagan centurion that Jesus said he had not found such faith in all Israel (Luke 7.9).

Further, it might seem strange to some people that the supreme reality should – so far as it is possible – disclose itself so significantly through a man. In reply we might ask, through what other existing creature could it better be disclosed? If in the future man evolves into superman or if there are higher creatures on other planets, then there is no reason, as far as I can see, why further utterance of God should not come through them. But for us that time has not come; though it may well be:

> God has other Words for other worlds,
> But for this world the Word of God is Christ.

Secondly, is there adequate historical evidence on which to base this claim for Jesus Christ? I would agree with Rudolf Bultmann that a study of the documents alone 'can only bring us to an encounter with Jesus as a phenomenon of past history'[17], and not to faith in the living Christ. Yet this study can, I think, show that the step of faith is not unreasonable. For Jesus' first followers, we can see, the step of faith was almost certainly not wishful thinking. Their faith came as something quite contrary to their previous prejudices and presuppositions. These had one by one to be overturned by their own experience of Jesus. Their ingrained, rigidly defined monotheism ('God is God, and

87

man is man, and never the twain shall meet') was violently opposed to giving any divine honour to Jesus. The 'gods many and lords many' (1 Cor. 8.5 f.) of other nations was an idea abhorrent to these Jews. Then their conception of Messiah as a victorious leader had to be shattered by Christ's understanding of himself as a suffering Messiah: this is clear from Peter's outburst at Caesarea Philippi (Mark 8.27–33). Next, when Jesus was crucified, they thought it was all over, the Easter event took them by surprise.[18] Finally, in a remarkably few years his followers came not only to pray to him as a glorified Lord but to know him as an inclusive personality who incorporated them all into himself: 'You are all one person in Christ Jesus' (Gal. 3.28). It was a rapid road, but also for them a very hard road, by which they came to acknowledge Jesus Christ as one who 'was in the form of God' and who 'did not count equality with God as a thing to be grasped' (Phil. 2.6). This hard road to faith means, I think, that the seeker today for truth should weigh up very seriously this claim that is made about Christ.

Thirdly, there is the question about the essential content of Christ's disclosure. It is not primarily his teaching. Most of his sayings can be found in other teachers. The details are not very original. Yet, when it is taken together, it has a balance, depth and incisiveness which put Jesus as a teacher in a class by himself.

What takes us nearer to the heart of his disclosure are two things recorded in the gospels; first what he said about his vocation and about himself; and secondly the titles there used of him, such as Son of Man and Son of God. The precise significance of these two matters cannot be rapidly sorted out. Nor, as we have seen, can we be sure how much of the gospel material came from his lips in his lifetime and how much came out of subsequent reflection. But anyone who wishes to know who Christ is and what he discloses must give careful thought to these matters in the gospels.[19]

But indisputably the heart of Christ's disclosure is seen

in the total impact of his life, death and resurrection on the first Christians. Two things stand out in this impact, his demand for genuineness and his undefeatable love. First he exposed religious complacency, challenged authority and defied convention, not least by the company he kept. Of course other prophets and reformers have done and do this. But Jesus did it in an unparalleled way. There was no hardness or sense of superiority in his attack. For, secondly, it was all inspired and made possible by an unceasing love. At all moments he was, in Bonhoeffer's phrase, 'the man for others'. When his love, as love often does, drew upon itself the envy and resentment of the unloving, Jesus went steadily and firmly on. There was an 'astonishing sovereignty with which Jesus confronted men in his words and his actions'),[20] but it was the sovereignty of truthfulness and love. His love fortified him to go through misrepresentation, suffering and death itself. But love triumphed over jealousy and death. That was the victory of Easter. This is what assures us that the search for authenticity and the dynamic of unquenchable love are the way to live in fellowship with ultimate reality. Jesus, we may then conclude, is a unique – inclusively unique – disclosure of ultimate reality. This is the good news. We may put it, if we wish, as Dr Ogden does: Jesus is 'the final reality of God's love that confronts us as sovereign gift and demand in all the events of our existence'.[21]

But the New Testament says that this good news should be proclaimed not only by the words of the gospels, which all men are not prepared to read, but also through the life of the Christian *koinonia* which all should be able to see. Its grave failure in love – and all Christians share in this failure – is the infidelity and tragedy of the church. But the fact of this failure brings to all who are seeking reality and genuineness an invitation to live a life of persistent concern and love and, as far as their integrity allows, in the Spirit of Christ-among-his own. It is worth remembering that:

> Faith is not assent to a set of propositions, however true, but commitment to an ongoing movement of love grounded in the universe and expressed in Jesus Christ.[22]

Methods

This, then, seems to me to be the purpose for us of the scriptures and the heart of the good news they convey. But how can we make the best use of these scriptures in practice? There is no one way. We each need to explore for ourselves. I will sketch four ways which overlap with one another.

First, the words of Scripture are still able to speak to individuals with a simple self-authenticating power. I would like to cite the experience of two very different men, whom I know and greatly respect. Strangely enough it was Mark, the earliest gospel, which spoke to each. One was Antony Bloom, now archbishop to the Russian Orthodox Church in Britain. While a student in Paris he had lost his faith. Under pressure he went in a surly manner to hear a lecture on Christ and Christianity. The rest must be told in his own words:

> I hurried home in order to check the truth of what the lecturer had been saying. I asked my mother whether she had a book of the gospels because I wanted to know whether the gospel would support the monstrous impression I had derived from this talk. I expected nothing good from my reading, so I counted the chapters of the four gospels to be sure that I read the shortest, not to waste time unnecessarily. And thus it was the gospel according to St Mark which I began to read. I do not know how to tell you what happened. I will put it quite simply and those of you who have gone through a similar experience will know what came to pass. While I was reading the beginning of St Mark's gospel, before I reached the third chapter, I was aware of a presence. I saw nothing. I heard nothing. It was no hallucination. It was a simple certainty that the Lord was standing there and that I was in the presence of him whose life I had begun to read with such revulsion and such ill-will.

The other is a man of a different temperament and of a different tradition, an Anglican layman, Sir John Lawrence. He had been brought up in a liberal Christian family and had read Greats at Oxford. He has written of his subsequent experience:

> When the last glow (of faith) had faded from the horizon, the world seemed by contrast inexpressibly cold and dreary. I was actually unhappy for a short time. Then I considered the fact that if nothing was proved, equally nothing was disproved. Ought I not to look again at Christian belief? So I got out my Greek Testament and began to read St Mark's gospel, a few verses a day. When I was about half way through I began to ask myself, 'Who then was Jesus?' Was he more than a man? After that I was over the top of the hill.

These are highlights: but such things happen to intelligent people in our century.[23]

Secondly, if anyone means to use the Bible effectively in his exploration of living and praying, he must know the main stream of the events which the Bible records and interprets. No one can really understand the significance of particular biblical passages unless he sees them in their original setting in the history of the Jewish people or in the life of the early Christian communities. The best small introduction I know is Professor C. H. Dodd's *The Bible Today*, a series of open lectures given in Cambridge. After one introductory book I would suggest reading the documents themselves, or rather selected passages with brief notes. Bishop Stephen Neill has produced two masterly three-month reading courses.[24] There is also excellent choice of passages, arranged in chronological order with brief notes, in the *Oxford Shorter Bible*. One of the values of following the selected passages in a daily office (as described in chapter 5) is that it gives us year by year this panoramic view of the Bible. Dietrich Bonhoeffer stressed the importance of *lectio continua*, consecutive reading, and this is what he did in prison.[25] The aim of this kind of reading is not to acquire dry-as-dust knowledge about dates of the kings of Israel and Judah or the places Paul visited, nor to find pat answers to today's problems, but to help us to participate in that history which reached

91

a high point of vitality in those early groups where Christ was experienced among-his-own. Professor Dodd sums this up:

The Bible is offered to us by the church as a revelation of God; not, certainly, as a sort of inspired encyclopaedia, where chapter and verse can be turned up and questions settled out of hand. On the contrary, it first makes us aware of the depth and the range of our problem, rooted as it is in the remote but still living past. *It plunges us into the stream of history* in a peculiarly significant part of its course. It makes present to us crucial events of the past by which the stream cuts for itself the channel in which it still sweeps us along. The biblical history is meaningful because it is related at every point to the fundamental reality which lies behind all history and all human experience, which is the living God in his kingdom; and because it moves towards a climax in which the Kingdom of God came upon men with conclusive effect.[26]

Thirdly, there is the way of linking Bible-reading with the kind of time of reflection recommended in chapter 3. The passage is not expected to throw immediate light on the day's work and pleasures, but it helps to keep life in a realistic perspective and to give that resilience which comes from participating in the experience of other men of faith. A useful book for this purpose is *Letters to Young Churches* by J. B. Phillips, which has opened to many people a new world.

These three ways of using the Bible have a limitation: they are quite individualistic. To balance them I would like to suggest a fourth method, something more corporate. This will link up with what has been said earlier in this book about the importance of small groups in our present situation both for seekers and for believers. We know the first Christians met in small groups in one another's houses. It was to groups like these that the epistles were originally read. What lively discussions must have been triggered off by what we call the First Letter to the Corinthians! (There had been earlier correspondence.) The raw materials which have been worked into our gospels probably came out of conversations in the early Christian groups, as they

92

exchanged and talked over their recollections of the Lord.

What confronts us immediately and directly in the New Testament documents is simply and only the primitive community – what it remembered, what it knew, what it thought, what it felt about Jesus.[27]

This method of reflection could be used for almost any part of the New Testament. Certain parts of the Old Testament, like the poem about the suffering servant of the Lord in Isaiah 53 or some of the psalms, would also be suitable material.

My suggestion would be that one should start with a little silence. Some might wish to remember 'Christ-among-his-own'; all would probably be glad of a moment to 'unwind'. Then a passage, preferably agreed on beforehand, would be read. One or two points might need preliminary elucidation. The discussion, I think, should not be technically academic, though I hope it would be based on good scholarship. It would be quite a free discussion. But three basic questions might often be asked – How did the first Christians feel about problems in their own situation which might be raised by this passage? What light was thrown for them on these issues by the life, death and resurrection of Christ? Did their own past experience of 'life in the Spirit' have any bearing on what they should do next? In such a discussion we might see how to make allowance for the 'personal equations' of the original observers and writers, and we might help one another to locate our own 'blind spots' in biblical reflection. But the dicussion should not be left to the more theologically articulate; everyone should offer his own reflections. This is a time to share reflections, to respect the opinions of others – and not to enter into high-powered debate. Nor, as we have seen, must we expect precise solutions for twentieth-century problems from first-century documents. After this discussion probably another and a longer time of silence would be appreciated. Personal reflection is important. There should be time enough to come to some kind of decision, if any wish to do so. It might often be a private and individual decision. But at times some corporate decision might well emerge, perhaps to carry out some piece of local service, perhaps to make some considered protest, perhaps to give encouragement to some other group by offering to collaborate with them in some action.

The New Testament itself is both the inspiration of and the record of a new upsurge of vitality, which broke into the world through the Christ event and the consequent life in the Spirit in the early Christian communities. If Christians today can rediscover how to reflect upon and how to be reactivated by this New Testament, then

> with such a book in its hand the church cannot fail to be adventurous – and to be prepared to see new things in our time, great and wonderful and unexpected, as the Spirit leads us where he will.[28]

NOTES

1. For an estimate of what help might be received from such sources see: J. A. Cuttah, 'Christian Experience and Oriental Spirituality'; W. Johnston, 'Dialogue with Zen'; D. H. Salman, 'Psychedelic Drugs and Religious Experience', all in *Concilium*, November 1969.

2. Günther Bornkamm, *Jesus of Nazareth*, London: Hodder and Stoughton, and New York: Harper and Row 1963, p. 15.

3. T. G. A. Baker, *What is the New Testament?*, London: SCM Press 1969, p. 21. For this chapter I owe a great deal to that book and to the writings of Professor John Knox, especially *The Church and the Reality of Christ*, New York: Harper and Row 1962, and London: Collins 1963.

4. John Knox, *The Early Church and the Coming Great Church*, New York: Harper, and London: Epworth Press 1957, p. 49 (italics mine). 'The Christ event' means the life, death and resurrection of the Lord, including in some sense their impact upon his early followers.

5. D. Sölle, *The Truth is Concrete*, London: Burns and Oates 1969, p. 28.

6. R. Bultmann, 'New Testament and Mythology', in: H. W. Bartsch (ed.), *Kerygma and Myth*, London: S.P.C.K. 1953, p. 21.

7. Compare John 10.10; 17.3.

8. M. Noth, *The History of Israel*, London: A. and C. Black, and New York: Harper 1960[2], p. 256.

9. L. S. Thornton, *Revelation and the Modern World*, London: Dacre Press 1950, p. 208.

10. W. D. Davies, *Invitation to the New Testament*, London: Darton, Longman and Todd 1967, p. 467.

11. Günther Bornkamm, *op. cit.*, pp. 21, 24, 25.

12. K. Stendahl, *The Bible and the Role of Women*, Philadelphia: Fortress Press 1966, p. 11; see also his article 'Biblical Theology (Contemporary)', *Interpreter's Dictionary of the Bible I*, New York: Abingdon Press 1962, pp. 418 ff.

13. T. G. A. Baker, *op. cit.*, p. 85.

14. For this phrase and for much of this section I am much indebted to an essay 'Is Christ Unique?' by Professor C. F. D. Moule in *Faith, Fact and Fantasy*, London: Fontana Books 1964, pp. 101–25.

15. Justin Martyr, *Apology II* xiii.

16. W. N. Pittenger, *God in Process*, London: SCM Press 1967, p. 105.

17. Rudolf Bultmann, 'A Reply to the Theses of J. Schniewind' *Kerygma and Myth*, p. 117.

18. See Mark 16.18; Luke 24.11, 31.37; Matt. 28.17; John 20.9, 25.

19. For further details see O. Cullmann, *The Christology of the New Testament*, London: SCM Press, and Philadelphia: Westminster Press 1963²; R. H. Fuller, *The Foundations of New Testament Christology*, London: Lutterworth Press 1965.

20. H. Zahrnt, *The Historical Jesus*, London: Collins 1963, p. 112.

21. S. M. Ogden, *Christ without Myth*, London: Collins 1962, p. 189.

22. W. N. Pittenger, *op. cit.*, p. 109.

23. These two passages are taken from a collection of autobiographical essays: R. E. Davis (ed.), *We Believe in God*, London: Allen and Unwin 1968, pp. 26, 115.

24. S. Neill, *Seeing the Bible Whole*, 1957, and *One Increasing Purpose*, 1969. Both are published by the Bible Reading Fellowship, 148 Buckingham Palace Road, London SW1, which issues various series of quarterly Bible-reading notes.

25. Dietrich Bonhoeffer, *Life Together*, pp. 40–45; *Letters and Papers from Prison*, pp. 45 f., 87 f.

26. C. H. Dodd, *The Bible Today*, Cambridge: The University Press 1946, pp. 13 f. Compare T. G. A. Baker, *What is the New Testament?*, p. 114.

27. John Knox, *The Church and the Reality of Christ*, p. 9.

28. F. C. Grant, *Introduction to New Testament Thought*, London: Faber, and New York: Abingdon Press 1950, p. 42.

7 Prayer of Asking

'There is only one thing I cannot accept in what you have said, and that is intercession. I cannot believe that my praying for other people is going to make any practical difference to them, unless conceivably it sets up some kind of telepathic thought transference between us.' This was said to me by an intelligent woman who was persuaded to come, rather reluctantly, to some addresses and discussions on prayer. She started the course practically from zero, she managed to assimilate a good deal of it, but intercession, as usually understood, remained an impossibility for her. She spoke, I think, for many inside as well as outside the Christian churches.

Misunderstandings

Now prayer is far wider than intercession. My advice is always, 'Use those kinds of prayer which are meaningful to you, try to use them to the full; leave the rest, and do not do anything contrary to your intellectual honesty.' Plenty of people can and do pray without interceding for others. Paul van Buren pinpoints their difficulty when he says that intercession 'in its traditional language leads them to imagine something which contradicts their empirical attitudes'.[1] But in this chapter we will take another look at intercession. We can begin by removing two misunderstandings, apparently implied by some traditional forms of prayer. These have needlessly put some people off from intercession.

First, we must be clear that believers think of intercession as something far more than giving God information or jogging his memory. Jesus – even if for the moment we regard him as no more than a highly gifted teacher of prayer – is recorded to have said 'Your father knows what your needs are before you ask him' (Matt. 6.8 NEB). Yet he himself interceded for people and encouraged others to do the same. In passing, we may notice that, if believers specify the needs of those for whom they pray, it is not to inform God; rather, these words well up from within them as an instinctive expression of the depth and sincerity of their concern; this, surely, is no bad thing.

The second misunderstanding is that some traditional practices of prayer look as if believers think they can talk God round and make him change his mind. Christian prayers cannot be like the frenzied prayers of the prophets of Baal on Mount Carmel, who cried out from morning to evening, 'O Baal, answer us'. The gospels make this very clear:

In your prayers do not go babbling on like the heathen, who imagine the more they say the more likely they are to be heard (Matt. 6.7 NEB)

Yet in spite of this clear teaching, we find Jesus himself, in the garden of Gethsemane, repeating his words of prayer and persevering in the effort of prayer; and he encouraged his followers to do the same; for example, he told the parable of the father woken up at midnight and the parable of the importunate widow, about whom the unjust judge said, 'This widow is so great a nuisance that I will see her righted before she wears me out with her persistence'.[2] These parables could be misinterpreted. Jesus cannot have intended to give the impression that God had to be woken up and have pressure put on him through prayer. Presumably he must have wished to encourage his followers to persevere in prayer, not to impress God but rather to deepen their own sense of dependence on God. How important this is in the life of prayer is well indicated by Archbishop William Temple:

What things are good for us may depend on our spiritual state. Food which is wholesome or nourishing for those who are in good health may be lethal poison to any who are in high fever. The worst of all diseases of the soul is detachment from God, whether by ignorance or by neglect. If all our wants are supplied while we have no thought of God, this may confirm us in our detachment from him.

We may not pray for anything except so far as we believe it to be God's will; but that belief is very fallible. The purpose of God's delay (in answering our prayer) may well be to detach our faith in him from all trust in our own judgement. Scarcely anything deepens and purifies faith in God for his own sake as surely as perseverance in prayer despite long disappointment.[3]

Probably no one has put this so succinctly and robustly as St Augustine:

God does not ask us to tell him our needs that he may learn about them, but in order that we may be capable of receiving what he is preparing to give.[4]

Reflex effect of prayer

Perhaps I have been pressing on a little too fast and skirting over difficulties. I am thinking now of those who are searching for a way of prayer which they can honestly use. I take seriously those who cannot see how praying for other people is going to make any practical difference to them. We all know well what appears most immediately to help other people; it is our actions, not our inward desires or prayers. But people are influenced not only by our deliberate actions, but also by our habitual attitude towards them. Many have become finer people through the silent influence of their companions and friends. There may be more in this than meets the eye. If, as I have suggested earlier in this book, God in his dynamic immanence upholds and penetrates all things and particularly all persons, then this good influence of a friend is also to some extent the flow through him of the divine energy and care. For this flow of human influence and probably also of divine care, we are all either channels or dams. We often fail to be channels, not through ill-will, but through lethargy, short-sightedness and lack of alertness. Perhaps for some of us, praying for others – or at least the beginning of praying for others – is finding out how to keep ourselves alert and alive to them and their needs.

So for those who cannot see how intercession can affect others, I would sugest that they now consider how intercession might influence indirectly but perceptibly the person himself who prays sincerely. I could give many instances of this. It is vividly and quaintly illustrated in a classic which I have mentioned already, *A Serious Call*, by the eighteenth-century scholar William Law:

> When Ouranius first entered into holy orders, he had a haughtiness in his temper, a great contempt and disregard for all foolish and unreasonable people. At his first coming to his little village it was as disagreeable to him as a prison, and every day seemed too tedious to be endured in so retired a place. He though his parish was too full of poor and mean people, that there were none fit for the conversation of a gentleman. This put him upon a close application to his studies. He kept much at home, writ notes upon Homer and Plautus, and sometimes thought it hard to be called to pray by any poor body when he was just in the midst of one of Homer's battles.
>
> This was his polite, or I may rather say poor, ignorant turn of mind before prayer had got the government of his heart. But now he presents every one of his parishioners so often before God in his prayer that he never thinks he can esteem reverence or serve those enough for whom he implores so many mercies from God. He now thinks the poorest creature in his parish good enough and great enough to deserve the humblest attendances, the kindest friendships, the tenderest offices he can possibly show them. These are the happy effects, which a devout intercession hath produced in the life of Ouranius.[5]

Empirical difficulties

We live in an empirical age. Everything must be tested, evidence must be carefully sifted. Even for men who believe in God – and in God in a personal sense – difficulties arise about intercession when it is examined empirically. Can you, they ask, actually prove that prayers are answered?

First, there is the problem that arises from the gigantic size of the universe as disclosed by modern astronomy. Man in comparison is so microscopic that his desires and prayers seem not to count for anything. For many people today this looks like an insuperable problem. But quietly considered it is seen to be not a difficulty for the reason but a difficulty of the imagination. It says in effect, 'You cannot imagine how'. The immensity of the universe mesmerizes human imagination. This difficulty really comes from picturing God in a naïve, anthropomorphic pagan way; and my reply must be ludicrously brief. The old pagans wrote, '*Magna di curant, parva negligunt*' – the gods care for the great things and neglect the small. This really adds up to imagining God as the director of the universe, so preoccupied with the big business of galaxies that he has no time left over to consider the rich, personal relationships of human creatures. This is contrary to the conception of God presented to us by contemporary theologians and sketched in this book; and it is clean contrary to all the insights brought to us by Jesus Christ.

A second difficulty arises from the scientific view of the universe in the following way: it is sometimes said that the scientific concept of the order of the universe rules out the possibility of events 'caused' by God in answer to prayer. But no scientist *qua* scientist would now say that the universe is a closed system governed by the inflexible laws of nature. The so-called laws of nature, if I understand them correctly, are no more and no less than shorthand summaries of a very large number of experiments and observations. If the scientific concept of these laws does not rule out the possibility of human choice and human initiatives, then logically it cannot rule out divine choice, initiative and action. How this divine action may take place in answer to prayer is another question, but its possibility cannot be denied on purely scientific grounds.

Thirdly, there is the problem of the strange distribution of apparently answered and unanswered prayers. Perhaps we can find no empirical answer to it. But we must in all honesty face it. To take a crude instance of an air crash. If on the crashed plane there was, let us say, a businessman who never prayed and who moved in a circle of people who never prayed, and also on the plane was a bishop, widely admired and very much prayed for, does it follow that the bishop will get off with less serious injuries than the businessman? Is it all a matter of chance or of prayer? Does God protect those who are prayed for, but not those who are not prayed for?

We can narrow this question down still further, though I realize that this may seem rather pernickety to some people. When a believer does not receive what he asks for, how can he know whether 'just nothing happened', or whether God deliberately said 'No' to his request? Of course he may come to see that his prayer was not answered, because it did not fulfil certain necessary preconditions – that, for example, his request was in fact egoistical or trivial, or that he did not ask with real confidence in God. But supposing all such preconditions were satisfied and yet God seemed not to answer 'Yes', how then can we be sure that God answered 'No', and not merely that nothing happened? The most we can say is this. If after this discouraging experience the man could say that this apparent lack of answer somehow deepened his relationship with God and his collaboration with God's purpose in the world, then it looks as if this really had been God's 'No', because such advancing of God's purpose in the world is the aim and object of all true prayer.

On the other side, when the request of prayer seems to be clearly answered, how can we be certain that this was not just a 'coincidence' which would have happened whether the man had prayed or not? Again this cannot be answered empirically. But if the 'answer' helped the man forward to a more generous service of God and his purpose, and if it opened his eyes to wider implications of this purpose, then we might feel confident that the answer was truly God's 'Yes'.

In brief, I would say that empirical investigation can neither disprove nor prove that intercession affects the person prayed for. How each one answers that question depends largely on what he thinks of the great men and women

101

of faith and prayer, and above all on what he thinks of the disclosure through Jesus Christ.

Jesus and intercession

If anyone thinks that Jesus is a reliable guide in this matter; further, if anyone thinks that Jesus is man, as mankind should and can be, then he must weigh up very seriously what Jesus said and did about prayer. Although the gospels are far from being a precise record of Christ's life, it is clear from them what his convictions were about prayer. He taught his followers to pray for others as well as for themselves, for today's bread as well as for today's forgiveness. If anyone can also accept what was suggested in the last chapter about Jesus as the disclosure of ultimate reality, as the disclosure of what can be known of God, and of what relationship man can have with God, then the life of Jesus will have even more persuasive power. We cannot overlook his early morning solitude for prayer, nor his nights of prayer, nor – even more – his daily sense of dependence on God in life and in prayer. If there is one thing certain about the teaching and personal attitude of Jesus, it is his direct sense of dependence on God. Rudolf Bultmann put this epigrammatically when he wrote, 'For Jesus, God became *a God at hand*'.[6] Professor Jeremias, from a minute examination of Jewish and early Christian documents, has shown that when Jesus spoke to God as *Abba*, his native Aramaic word expressing affectionate trust in a father, he went far beyond the attitude of a devout Jew of the first century; he brought a breath of fresh air into mankind's approach to God.

It was something new, something unique and unheard of, that Jesus dared to take this step and to speak with God as a child speaks with his father, simply, intimately, securely. There is no doubt, then, that the *Abba* which Jesus uses to address God reveals the very basis of his communion with God.[7]

And when Jesus gives his followers the Our Father, the Lord's prayer,

102

> He first and foremost authorized his disciples to follow him in saying *Abba*. He let them participate in his own communion with God. This address *Abba* is a sharing in his revelation. It is the presence of his kingdom even here, even now.[8]

Thus he offers to all who come to him – and often to those far outside the religious establishment – the opportunity to share in his fellowship with God and his concern for God's purpose for the world. The freshness and the intimacy of this Aramaic word *Abba* so struck the early Christians that they even retained it untranslated in their Greek prayers and writings.

Attitude of prayer

How, then, does prayer look, if we see it not as mere requests and answers, but in this wider context? Further, how might we consider setting about praying?

First, for those who may not be able to accept this biblical language – and perhaps not even what it symbolizes – I would suggest that they reflect on what they think man and human society should be, that is, the secular hope of today; next, that they look at the actual situation of men and women, particularly those who are round about them; then they should formulate their desire to involve themselves in changing the present situation; and finally decide, if possible, what they can do about it now. This is a simplified and personal form of *Nachtgebet*, outlined in chapter 4.

Those, on the other hand, who can in general accept the New Testament outlook, could do the same thing in a more explicitly Christian way. Christians hold that with the Christ event and the consequent life in the Spirit a great transformation has been inaugurated. Time will come, they believe, when believers will no longer be divided men, when the inner struggle between egoism and true love will be over, and when their love, strengthened by God's love, will be victorious. Time will come also, they think, when the jealousies and injustices of human society will be overcome. The reconciliation of Jew and Gentile in the early Christian communities is the first light of new dawn. The day will come, they firmly hope, when other unjust discriminations of colour and class, of sex and age, will be done away. Christ, by living, dying and rising has become the focus of this new humanity, he is creating out of these tough divisions 'a single new humanity in himself, thereby making peace' (Eph. 2.15 NEB). The New Testament Christians believed that by their union with Christ through believing, the transformation of individuals and society had already begun. 'When anyone is united to Christ, there is a new world; the old order has gone, and a new order has already begun' (II Cor. 5.17 NEB). They were not blind to facts. They saw clearly that the transformation had not yet been achieved; but it had already at least begun. They were living between the 'not yet' and the 'already'. They had to become what they were. They now looked forward to the achievement of this great hope, and they linked to it what they called the *parousia* or future coming of Christ. The biblical language about this may seem to us over-coloured and bizarre, but it is important to penetrate through the symbolism to the hope it symbolizes. Christians have hope not only for the individual believer, but also for the transformation of human society and of nature itself.

> He has made known to us his hidden purposes – such was his will and pleasure determined beforehand in Christ – to be put into effect when the time was ripe: namely, that the universe, all in heaven and on earth, might be brought into a unity in Christ (Eph. 1. 9f.)

Incidentally, this New Testament hope, while not identical with modern secular hope, could well underpin and give it strength and resilience in the inevitable times of disappointment and frustration.

It is against this background of the Christ event, the life in the Spirit and the New Testament hope that Christians should live and work, and hope and pray for their friends and neighbours and for the world today. What this means has been worked out in detailed and practical terms by Peter Baelz in his recent Hulsean lectures at Cambridge:

104

Prayer is no compulsive figment of the imagination, by which we pretend that things are not what they really are, and dream that they might be what we should like them to be. It is a contemplation of their present actuality within the context of the reality of the eternal purposes of God, such as we have reason to believe these to be. It is a seeing of the world and of our neighbour in the light of the new creation in Christ and in the confidence that the spirit of God lays hold upon our spirit and informs our hearts and minds. In prayer we learn to participate in the mind and action of God. . . .

Because it flows from a recognition of what God has already done in and through Jesus Christ, prayer will always have the note of thanksgiving. Because it looks forward to what God has still to do in and through those who respond to his love, it will also have the note of petition and intercession. . . .

Just as we have insisted that Christian prayer is an anticipation of the *parousia*, so we must regard it as only an anticipation. Christian prayer as well as Christian life is involved in and conditioned by the actualities of the world as it is. There is no magical transformation which ignores the conditions of history and of nature as they have come to be. There is in prayer itself the same tension between the 'already' and the 'not yet' as we have seen in the rest of Christian experience. The believer's offering of prayer is not yet the perfect response to God of obedience, wisdom and love. He offers it, therefore, in the name of the One whose response was perfect. He associates his offering with the perfect offering of Christ. . . .

And because of the tension between the 'already' and the 'not yet' a deliberate persistence in prayer is as important as a heart-felt but transient desire to pray. God is 'more ready to hear than we to pray'. A disposition to pray, or a habitual recollection of God, is developed by determinate and deliberate acts of prayer. These latter need not substitute a regimen of duties for an adventure of love, as love itself knows and creates its own disciplines. Spontaneity and order are mutually self-supporting.[9]

Prayer and action

It may still be difficult even for some Christians to understand how this intercession is going to work, and how it will help others. We are all clear that our love and our care may help others. Perhaps we could go further and say that we can conceive that God may use our love and concern in deeper ways than we can see. If he can use our concern, may he not use the desires and prayers which are an expres-

105

sion of that concern? When we pray for others, perhaps we are opening our lives to the love, concern and ongoing purpose of God, so that his purpose may be helped forward by our desires and love and in ways wider than we can at present grasp.

Genuine prayer for others cannot be divorced from care and action for them, any more than it was in the life of Jesus:

A man's prayer is not a mere message sent to God, voicing a request. It carries him with it deep into all that costly action which is the purpose of God in the life of the world.[10]

But prayer is more than costly action to help others. Prayer has moments of stepping out of the stream of activity and concern for others. This is not time lost or wasted. This is the opportunity to try to set our caring in its true perspective. For it is only too obvious that we can be active and concerned for others in mistaken ways. We need from time to time to try to realign our care for them with what seems to be the ongoing purpose of God, the great reality, disclosed to us particularly in Jesus Christ. Prayer is a redirecting of the desires and service of our lives, a representative dedication to the true good of others of the total help we can give. An Anglican theologian, Dr Oliver Quick, once spoke of prayer in this way:

True intercession must spring from a constant love for and desire to help the person for whom the intercession is made. This love and desire is itself a potential activity, and, if opportunity arises, it will issue in various forms of action besides the activity of prayer. This whole activity of help, whether it issue only in prayer, or in prayer and outward act as well, must be dedication to God and can only be effective as fulfilling His will. The significance and value of the particular activity of intercession now becomes obvious. It is simply a representative dedication to God of the total help which we give or desire to give, constantly and in varying forms, to the person for whom we intercede. My petition is simply an attempt to put my own feeble efforts of action and desire, frustrated as they are by the barriers of human and mortal limitation, into the hands of One who is surely able by their means to bring about the fulfilment after which they strive. Our theory leads us up to wider interpretations of the nature of prayer whereby religious thinkers ancient and modern have extended its range far beyond those times in which we consciously set ourselves to pray. It will follow that the secular activities of our life will constitute the very substance and matter of what we offer in our prayer.[11]

If prayer is seen as widely as this, it cannot be regarded only as personal communion between God and ourselves. It seeks to interweave our concerns for one another and for society with what we can discern of the ongoing divine purpose. The help we ask for seems to come, not outside of, but through this web of human relationship. Prayer is participation in the building up of the new humanity.

NOTES

1. Paul van Buren, *The Secular Meaning of the Gospel*, New York: The Macmillan Company, and London: SCM Press 1963, p. 190.

2. See Mark 14.32–41; Luke 11.5–8; 18.1–5.

3. William Temple, *Readings in St John's Gospel*, London: Macmillan 1963 (paperback), pp. 289 f.

4. St Augustine, *Letters* cxxx (to Flora) 17.

5. William Law, *A Serious Call*, London: Macmillan 1898, ch. 21, pp. 259 ff.

6. R. Bultmann, *Theology of the New Testament* I, London: SCM Press, and New York: Charles Scribner's Sons 1952, p. 23 (my italics).

7. J. Jeremias, *The Central Message of the New Testament*, London: SCM Press 1965, p. 21.

8. *Op. cit.*, pp. 28 f.; see also J. Jeremias, *The Prayers of Jesus*, London: SCM Press 1967.

9. P. R. Baelz, *Prayer and Providence*, pp. 100–102. The present chapter owes a great deal to this book.

10. J. Neville Ward, *The Use of Praying*, London: Epworth Press 1967, pp. 88 f.

11. O. C. Quick, *Essays in Orthodoxy*, London: Macmillan 1916, pp. 287–89.

8 Reality in Praying

Laurens van der Post's *Lost World of the Kalahari* is one of the most engrossing travel books I have ever read, and I have read hundreds. His forefathers had driven the aboriginal bushmen out of South Africa. He jotted down in his diary as a boy, 'I have decided today, when I am grown up, I am going into the Kalahari desert to seek out the bushmen.' He did not get round to it. Many circumstances including war-service prevented him carrying out his plan, but it was never for very long completely forgotten. 'Then one morning,' he wrote later in his book, 'I woke to find in sleep, my mind had been decided for me, I will go and find the bushmen.' Quickly and thoroughly his plans were made. He set out from the Zambesi river at the Victoria Falls, 'the smoke that thunders', as the Africans call its columns of spray. Then he drove in landrovers into the heart of the Kalahari desert. There was a momentary hesitation and delay before they started, until one of his companions said, 'There is only one time to start this sort of journey; not when you feel like it, but when you are ready for it.' In the Kalahari desert they had their difficulties, not least personal difficulties with the exploring party. Van der Post has called one chapter of his account 'The Swamp of Despond'; and he recorded, 'I have found that frequently one has to go down into what one most fears and in the process, from somewhere beyond all conscious expectation, comes a saving flicker of light and energy.' The exploration went on, and in the end van der Post was able to give to the world his fascinating account of the daily life of the bushmen with their surviving cave art and their joyful music-making. The whole book reads like the exploration and engagement in life through prayer.[1]

Prayer and feelings

Whether we have always prayed from childhood onwards or whether we start, or restart, later on, perhaps with some spurt of enthusiasm, we all run into dull patches. Of course, it is the same with everything, whether it is learning to play a musical instrument, or studying a language or making a real friendship. We know in these other activities that the only thing is to carry on and not to let ourselves be discouraged. But people become worried about these dull patches in prayer, common as they are. In fact I can only remember talking to two Christians who never had these discouraging periods; and oddly enough they were worried because they did not have these difficulties, which most of the books on prayer said that they would have. I spend many hours listening to clergy and laypeople saying, 'Prayer has gone dead for me. I do not know why. It seems so unreal. I feel a fraud and hypocrite when I try to pray.' The normal advice, at least in the general catholic tradition of the church to which I belong, is, 'Just carry on and don't bother about your feelings'. This was put in a striking way by Frank Weston, a good theologian, a first-rate missionary, the Bishop of Zanzibar in the tropics for sixteen years early in this century. I had quite forgotten his words, until by some trick of association van der Post's African book brought them back to memory. Frank Weston wrote – and he certainly practised in his endlessly demanding life what he taught – that the real art of prayer is 'to cling on with your will, when your heart is dead and your mind won't work'.[2]

On the whole I still think that that is good advice, because this clinging on is not clinging on to routine, but clinging on to Christ, and it is with him that we can often better help others. But I should wish now to qualify this advice a little. First, this tripartite division of man is artificial and will not do; there is an interlocking of will with heart and mind. Secondly, there is something in the contention of many young people today, who say that the love for man or God is unauthentic unless at times you actually feel it. To love God with your will when your heart is dead sounds like nonsense to them. 'They personify man's ancient thirst to taste both the holy and the human with unmediated directness.'[3] Thirdly, in the New Testament prayer is not something cold and unfelt. Dr John Knox is right when he says about those first small groups, 'Christian community is sharing of a common experience of the Spirit' and that was something felt, something tangible.[4] Paul asked the Christians in Galatia, who were now being tempted to switch to a legalistic religion, 'Answer me one question: did you receive the Spirit by keeping the law or by believing the gospel message? Have all your great experiences been in vain?' (Gal. 3.2–4)

I would now say that normally prayer should be felt. Heart, mind and will should be brought into play together. It will not always be like this, as experience clearly shows. But if it is never or very seldom like this, it is not right just to carry on, forcing yourself by your will. You should try to find out if anything has gone wrong. Lovers and partners in marriage also know that they cannot always live on the same level of deep feeling; but, if 'coldness' persists for months and years, surely they should enquire together into its root cause.

Underlying causes

When people come to me, as a Christian and as a priest, because they are concerned with this feeling of unreality in their prayers, I am inclined in the course of the conversation to raise one or more of five matters.

First, I would try to see if prayer had become a mere routine. I would suggest looking at prayer from a fresh angle; just as in a course of studies or in the pattern of married love light from a new angle or a new approach will

110

often bring fresh vitality into what was becoming stagnant. Michel Quoist's book *Prayers of Life* does not suit everyone, but it has renewed so many people's praying because it gave them a jolt and helped them to enter into prayer in a new way. Unless we are alert, prayer can all too easily become a routine and a burden. The writings of Teilhard de Chardin have kept many people alert and set them free from a legalistic routine. He wrote that prayer

is not, as it is sometimes presented and sometimes practised, an additional burden of observances and obligations to weigh down and increase the already heavy load, or multiply the already paralysing ties of our life in society. It is, in fact, a source of immense power which bestows significance and beauty and a new lightness on what we are already doing.[5]

Prayer is sometimes not words but silence, which, as between friends, speaks more profoundly than words. This silence, like love, is good in itself and for itself; though afterwards we have more to take into the world. Many people have discovered this in a few days spent quietly alone or with others. There are plenty of places now where this can be arranged.[6]

Secondly, praying sometimes dries up, because we are not really facing the underlying intellectual questions. Many people now have to live and earn their living in a very sceptical atmosphere. They cannot evade being faced with problems and perplexities. This is not necessarily a bad thing. It may refine faith and make it more adult. To turn away from these worrying questions in fear or to try to suppress your anxiety about them is dangerous. For in this way a man may preserve his pattern of prayer intact, but it can then easily become a rather hard, superficial programme of prayer. Possibly one day it will suddenly crack, or alternatively it may make him hard and aggressive about his religious practice. Many of us know how spiritually damaging it is to have to use forms of prayer which we cannot any longer accept intellectually. In corporate worship we have necessarily to accommodate ourselves to this kind of situation, because in any large group of worshippers there is certain nowadays to be a wide variety of theological views. Some kind of personal reinterpretation of traditional words of worship has always been recognized; even so, we ought to see to it that not too much ingenuity is demanded of us. But in personal prayer, though admittedly forms of prayer are often of a poetic or symbolical nature, intellectual integrity is vital. For our spiritual health we also need someone or some small group with whom we can discuss these questions humbly and frankly.

Thirdly, our physical health has a good deal to do with our praying, just as it does with the quality of our work or of our personal relationships. We ought to be particularly on our watch for various kinds of psychosomatic lethargy, which takes the joy and vivacity out of life and out of prayer. I cannot develop this here, but it would have been inexcusable not to mention it.

Fourthly, there clearly must be a basic harmony and integrity between our living and our praying. We need not exaggerate or be depressed about our minor and impulsive failings. Scrupulosity seldom ever does any good. But it is a different matter when a serious deliberate discrepancy is allowed to develop between our praying and our attempts to live up to our ideals. Excessive introspection is no help. But a life which is not reflected on and examined is less than a fully human life. We all need from time to time to check, to correct and to reset our course. If there is one thing that the New Testament makes clear, it is that we need no longer be weighed down by a sense of failure and remorse at our past faults. The first Christians knew the joy of being released from the burden of a heavy past. Dietrich Bonhoeffer worked out this truth in the last chapter of his book, *Life Together*. He also showed out of his own personal experience how we sometimes need another Christian to help us to realize the certainty and completeness of forgiveness.

Christ gave his followers the authority to hear the confession of sin and to forgive in his name. Christ became our Brother in order to help us. Now our brother has been given to us to help us. He hears the confession of our sins in Christ's stead and he forgives our sins in Christ's name. He keeps the secret of our confession as God keeps it. When I go to my brother to confess, I am going to God.[7]

In these problems of reality in prayer, some people may need skilled psychiatric aid. I am not writing now about that, but about the removing of hindrances to authentic prayer through forgiveness. In many traditions a fellow Christian is used in different ways to assure us that God has forgiven us and that the road to living prayer is open.

Charles de Foucauld was brought up in a Catholic school, but he drifted far from any Christian believing or living in the French army; in Algeria he was removed from the active list because he would not send back to France his mistress, who was calling herself his wife, the Vicomtesse de Foucauld. Once he was out of the army, disguised as a Jewish rabbi he explored Morocco, then closed to foreigners. Impressed by the religious practice of the Moslems, he came back to France with the strange prayer on his lips, 'My God, if you exist, grant me to know you'. One morning he went to a confessional in a Paris church, he knew the priest a little and he murmured, 'I have not come to confession, I have no faith'. The priest, Abbé Huvelin – perhaps not one priest in a thousand would have dared or have had the insight to say it – quietly remarked, 'It is not your faith, my friend, but your conscience that is at fault'. Charles confessed and was absolved. The block had been removed and now he would have no half-measures in his commitment to Christ. He became the inspiration of the Little Brothers and the Little Sisters. Though he was killed in Algeria in the First World War, his words speak directly to the men and women of our day.[8]

Fifthly, what keeps prayer from becoming living prayer is not always the past, but rather the fear of the future. People sometimes fear that, if they let themselves go in prayer, they will be carried much further than they bargained for. We understand this, because there is, of course, at times a similar fear in a growing friendship or love. A modern writer on prayer has said, 'Prayer is not possible for a person who is too insecure to trust.'[9] I could not go so far as that, but there is something in what he says.

Carrying on

Helping others means listening to them. Somewhere in the conversations about unreality in prayer these five issues are likely to crop up. If none of them seems to explain the lack of feeling in prayer, it may then very well be that for a time this dried-up feeling must be accepted philosophically and, if possible, cheerfully. It may even be a necessary stage in the growth of real prayer. Great men and women of prayer have had this testing. Dietrich Bonhoeffer, in the darkness of his last years of prison life, wrote, 'The God who is with us is the God who forsakes us. Before God and with God we live without God';[10] yet he continued praying day by day in his cell.

This experience may at present be beyond us. But we have all seen many good initiatives in sport, in education, or in social service lose their impetus, when the initial enthusiasm slackens and when it has not been underpinned with real determination. It is right that spontaneity and enthusiasm should play an important part in life and in prayer. But important concerns cannot wait for times when our feelings are stirred. Love has spontaneity, but it also finds its own *disciplined* strength. Bonhoeffer again insisted on the necessity of the 'hidden discipline'.[11]

This needs to be said clearly to all who would wish to find strength and reality in prayer. Some people find at certain times a satisfaction and joy in prayer; this is something to be glad about. It is like an exhilarating summer holiday, hiking across a continent, or camping by the woods and the sea, or living amongst the mountains. But this does not really make you a lover of other nations or of nature or of the mountains. For that you need to face life and nature in all its moods, in sun and in cloud, in wind or in storm –

unless you wish to be a mere tourist and not a lover. Too many people have been led to think that religious feelings and the reality of praying are almost the same thing, as if the excitement of one's first romance were the same thing as deep, proved partnership of trust and love. In all human friendship, love and companionship, there are high moments; there are uneventful, rather dull, patches; and there may be times of what seems almost dead unresponsiveness. It is, I suppose, by working through *all* these experiences together that human friends and lovers come to real depth in their relationship with one another and so make of their friendship and love a joy and strength for others.

So it is, I believe, with reality in praying.

NOTES

1. Laurens van der Post, *The Lost World of the Kalahari*, Harmondsworth: Penguin Books 1962, pp. 61, 67, 100, 171.

2. H. Maynard Smith, *Frank, Bishop of Zanzibar*, London: SPCK 1926, p. 142. This biography may in some ways be dated, but it shows what serving and praying means.

3. Harvey Cox, *Feast of Fools*, p. 102

4. John Knox, *The Church and the Reality of Christ*, p. 61.

5. Pierre Teilhard de Chardin, *Le Milieu Divin*, p. 70.

6. The Association for Promoting Retreats, 23 Victoria Grove, London W8, publish twice a year a list of centres and of retreats.

7. Dietrich Bonhoeffer, *Life Together*, pp. 101 f.

8. Roger Voillaume, *Brothers of Men: Letters to the Little Brothers from their Prior*, London: Darton, Longman and Todd 1966, pp. 8 f.

9. J. Neville Ward, *The Use of Praying*, London: Epworth Press 1967, p. 143.

10. Dietrich Bonhoeffer, *Letters and Papers from Prison*, p. 196.

11. By 'hidden discipline' Bonhoeffer seems to mean both (i) a proper reticence in using the traditional words of the Christian faith in situations where they might be seriously misunderstood and also (ii) a secret, flexible discipline of prayer, which is a channel of strength to maintain our living as Christians in the world. We see both of these principles in his own life.

Appendix A

	Thanksgiving	*Intercessions*
Monday	Creation and providence	The world: peace, racial understanding
Tuesday	Revelation and human knowledge	Society: employment, education, research
Wednesday	Personal relationships	Reconciliation and human relationships
Thursday	God's gifts through the church	Church: its unity, renewal and mission
Friday	All that meets human need	Those who suffer
Saturday	The present signs of the fulfilment of God's purpose	Sick and departed

Appendix B

A Eucharistic Liturgy

As prepared by the People and Clergy of St Mark's-in-the-Bouwery, New York, for use on special ecumenical occasions

The Preparation

Celebrant	*We are here.*
Assembly	In the name of Jesus Christ.
Celebrant & Assembly	We are here because we are men – but we deny our humanity. We are stubborn fools and liars to ourselves. We do not love others. We war against life. We hurt each other. We are sorry for it and know we are sick from it. We seek new life.
Celebrant	*Giver of life, heal us and free us to be men.*
Celebrant & Assembly	Holy Spirit, speak to us. Help us to listen for we are very deaf. Come, fill this moment.

Silence for a Time

The Service of the word

Old Testament Lesson

Psalm

Epistle

Hymn

The Gospel

Sermon

Intercessions

THE OFFERTORY

The celebrant shall begin the offertory with the following words:

> *If you are offering your gift at the altar, and there remember that your brother has something against you, leave your gift at the altar and go, first be reconciled to your brother, and then come and offer your gift* (Matt. 5.23).

After which he will turn to the deacon first and then the reader saying:

> *Peace, my friend*

And the deacon shall answer:

> *Peace*

Then the deacon and reader will give the 'Peace' to the congregation.

Then the celebrant shall read the following words:

> *I appeal to you therefore, brethren, by the mercies of God, to present your bodies as a living sacrifice, holy and acceptable to God, which is your spiritual worship. Do not be conformed to this world, but be transformed by the renewal of your mind, that you may prove what is the will of God, what is good and acceptable and perfect* (Rom. 12.1–2).

A hymn

THE ACT OF THANKSGIVING

Celebrant	*Lift up your hearts.*
Assembly	We lift them to the Lord.
Celebrant	*Let us give thanks for God's glory.*
Assembly	We give thanks: we rejoice in the glory of all creation.

Celebrant	*All glory be to you, O Father, who sent your only Son into the world to be a man, born of a woman's womb, to die for us on a cross that was made by us.*
Assembly	He came for us. Help us to accept his coming.
Celebrant	*He walked among us, a man, on our earth, in our world of conflict, and commanded us to remember his death, his death which gives us life; and to wait for him until he comes again in glory.*
Assembly	We remember his death. We live by his presence; we wait for his coming.
Celebrant	*On the night he was betrayed, the Lord Jesus took bread, he gave thanks; he broke it, and gave it to his disciples, saying, 'Take, eat: this is my body. Do this in remembrance of me'. He also took the cup; he gave thanks, and gave it to them, saying, 'Drink of it, all of you; this is my blood of the covenant, which is poured out for many for the forgiveness of sins'.*
Assembly	Come, Lord Jesus, come.
Celebrant	*Therefore, remembering his death, believing in his rising from the grave, longing to recognize his presence; now, in this place, we obey his command; we offer bread and wine, we offer ourselves, to be used.*
Assembly	Everything is yours, O Lord; we return the gift which first you gave us.
Celebrant	*Accept it, Father. Send down the Spirit of life and power, glory and love, upon these people, upon this bread and wine, that to us they may be his body and his blood.*
Assembly	Come, risen Lord, live in us that we may live in you.
Celebrant	*Now with all men who ever were, are, and will be, with all creation in all time, with joy we sing,*
Celebrant & Assembly	Holy, holy, holy, Lord God almighty, all space and all time show forth your glory now and always. Amen.

Celebrant   *And now, in his words, we are bold to say:*
             The Lord's prayer.

Then shall the celebrant break the bread before the assembly, saying:

             The gifts of God for the people of God.
             Amen.

THE COMMUNION

For the bread shall be said:

Celebrant   *The Body of Christ.*
Assembly   Amen.

For the wine shall be said:
Celebrant   *The Blood of Christ.*
Assembly   Amen.

A hymn may be sung.

THE DISMISSAL

Celebrant   *Go. Serve the Lord. You are free.*
Assembly   Amen.

For Further Reading

P. R. Baelz, *Prayer and Providence*, SCM Press 1968.

B. C. Butler, *Prayer, an Adventure in Living*, Darton, Longman and Todd 1961.

Rex Chapman, *A Kind of Praying*, SCM Press 1970.

Eric James (ed.), *Spirituality for Today*, SCM Press 1968.

M. Nédoncelle, *The Nature and Use of Prayer*, Burns and Oates 1964.

D. Z. Phillips, *The Concept of Prayer*, Routledge and Kegan Paul 1965.

Pierre Teilhard de Chardin, *Le Milieu Divin*, Fontana Books 1964.

J. N. Ward, *The Use of Praying*, Epworth Press 1967.

Simone Weil, *Waiting for God*, Routledge and Kegan Paul 1951.

Index

123